From
Vision to
Practice

From Vision to Practice

The Art of Educational Leadership

Richard C. Wallace, Jr.

CORWIN PRESS, INC.
A Sage Publications Company
Thousand Oaks, California

For information address:

Corwin Press, Inc.
A Sage Publications Company
2455 Teller Road
Thousand Oaks, California 91320
E-mail: order@corwin.sagepub.com

SAGE Publications Ltd.
6 Bonhill Street
London EC2A 4PU
United Kingdom

SAGE Publications India Pvt. Ltd.
M-32 Market
Greater Kailash I
New Delhi 110 048 India

Printed in the United States of America

Library of Congress Cataloging-in-Publication Data

Wallace, Richard C., Jr.
   From vision to practice: The art of educational leadership /
Richard C. Wallace, Jr.
      p.   cm.
   Includes bibliographical references and index.
   ISBN 0-8039-6157-X (cloth: alk. paper).—ISBN 0-8039-6158-8 (pbk.:
alk. paper)
   1. School management and organization—United States.   2. School
superintendents—United States.   3. Educational leadership—United
States.   4. Educational change—United States.   5. Educational
evaluation—United States.   I. Title.
LB2805.W3236   1995
371.2′00973—dc20   95-21340

This book is printed on acid-free paper.

96   97   98   99   10   9   8   7   6   5   4   3   2   1

Corwin Production Editor: Diana E. Axelsen
Corwin Typesetter: Andrea D. Swanson

Contents

Part II: Reform Initiatives and Educational Leadership

Preface

Written by a practitioner for practitioners, this book describes my perceptions of the superintendent as an educational leader and also provides examples of what educational leadership really means in practice. I intend to convey an image of a vision-based superintendent who seeks to improve the quality of education for students and the performance of teachers and administrators.

The emphasis is on leadership, for although management is an important part of the role and preparation of a superintendent, one must remember that management skills alone are not enough for those who face the challenge of educational reform.

This book contributes to the literature on superintendency. It reflects my 19 years as a superintendent as well as a total of 33 years of administrative experience spanning positions from principal to assistant superintendent as well as deputy director and director of educational research institutions, which took place in rural, suburban, small urban, and large urban communities and in a university setting.

Audiences for the Book

This is the work of a reflective practitioner. The primary audiences are practitioners interested in educational leadership in general and those aspiring to superintendency in particular. Practicing superintendents may find my ideas useful in clarifying their roles as educational leaders; they may also find the descriptions of programs helpful in making program adaptations in their school districts. Professors of educational administration may find this book a useful and practical supplement to textbooks on administrative theory.

The extended audiences would be all the constituencies who contribute to comprehensive educational reform in their districts. Included in this group are those who have been of assistance to me in my tenure as superintendent: teachers, principals, central office personnel, board members, union leaders, business leaders, foundation executives, parents, and the general public.

Contents of the Book

The book is organized in two parts. Part I (Chapters 1 through 6) conveys general principles of educational leadership gleaned from my experiences. Part II (Chapters 7 through 11) provides illustrations of applications of these principles, with examples of programs implemented in Pittsburgh, where I was superintendent from 1980 to 1992, and other exemplary programs from around the country. To maintain a degree of objectivity about programs in which I was directly involved, with minor exceptions, I have selected programs in Pittsburgh schools that have been recognized by national organizations or written about in books or publications. For example, the Arts PROPEL program described in Chapter 9 was identified by *Newsweek* in 1991 as one of the 10 best educational programs in the world; the Pittsburgh union and management collaboration, discussed in Chapter 7, was described by Kerchner and Koppich in their 1993 book, *A Union of Professionals*. Part II also describes selected programs in rural, suburban, and urban districts across the United States.

Some chapters in Part I are paired with some in Part II: Chapter 3 provides the principles and Chapter 8, examples of needs assessment surveys as the basis for developing a reform agenda. Chapter 4 describes principles to improve student achievement and assessment, and Chapter 9 illustrates corresponding efforts. Chapter 5 discusses the superintendent's role in professional development; Chapter 10 provides descriptions of exemplary staff development programs. Chapters 6 and 11 give the principles and examples of community involvement.

To briefly describe the remaining chapters, Chapter 1 deals with the concepts of vision and visionary leadership. It describes excellence in performance for all stakeholders of a school district as the basis for developing an excellence agenda and a strategic plan.

In Chapter 2, I talk about how a superintendent exercises educational leadership and the commitment it requires. This chapter points out that, to have the time to provide educational leadership, the superintendent will have to delegate much of the management responsibility to competent subordinates.

—RICHARD C. WALLACE, JR.

Acknowledgments

I am grateful to Joseph Calihan, president of the Calihan Foundation, for funds to support the research associate who gathered information for Part II. This grant allowed me to go beyond the boundaries of Pittsburgh to describe the effects of educational leadership in urban, suburban, and rural school districts around the country.

This book would not have been written without the collaboration, encouragement, and technical assistance of my wife, Rita Tessier Wallace, PhD. Her toleration of my 19 years as a superintendent allowed me to put into operation the role of superintendent as educational leader. Her extensive searches for exemplary programs was invaluable; her contacts with educational leaders across the country led to telephone conferences informing us of interesting and effective programs. Her preparation of reports on programs in school districts across the country was vital. Finally, her tireless editing of the book contributed significantly to its clarity of expression and completeness.

I am grateful to the following colleagues across the country who gave so willingly of their time and talent to talk about the exciting programs in their school districts: Donald Raczka, Poway, California; David Pratt,

Greece, New York; Dr. Daniel Challener and Dr. Edward Eddy, the PROBE Commission, Providence, Rhode Island; Barbara McKay, former director of the Public Education Fund in Providence, Rhode Island; Dr. Arthur Zarrella, superintendent, Providence, Rhode Island; Dr. Gregory Morris, Dr. Diane Briars, and JoAnne Eresh, Pittsburgh, Pennsylvania; Richard Durost, principal, Presque Isle High School, Presque Isle, Maine; Linda Anderson, principal, Ten Sleep High School, Ten Sleep, Wyoming; Dr. Marcetta Reilly, superintendent, Royal Valley, Kansas; Kathryn Blumsack, director of the School Improvement Unit and Karolyn Rohr, director of the Systemwide Training Unit, Montgomery County, Maryland; Dr. Mike Walters, superintendent, Tupelo, Mississippi; and Pamela Block, director, Northwest Suburban Career Cooperative, Palatine, Illinois.

In particular, I want to thank Charlene Travato and Stephanie Dobbler of the Superintendents Academy, University of Pittsburgh, for their technical assistance. I also thank the union and association leaders and my many colleagues, too many to mention, in the Pittsburgh Public Schools who provided me with the stimulation to expand and enrich my concept of the superintendent as an educational leader. I have been privileged to work with an incredibly competent and dedicated group of professionals.

I am grateful to the boards of education in Fitchburg, Massachusetts, and Pittsburgh, Pennsylvania, who gave me the opportunity to implement the role of the superintendent of education.

About the Author

Richard C. Wallace, Jr. is Superintendent Emeritus of the Pittsburgh, Pennsylvania, Public Schools; he is Clinical Professor of Educational Administration at the University of Pittsburgh, where he also serves as the Codirector of the Superintendents Academy. From 1980 to 1992, he led the Pittsburgh schools to a position of national and international prominence as an innovative urban school district. Programs such as the Schenley High School Teacher Center, Arts PROPEL, and Monitoring Achievement in Pittsburgh won awards or were recognized as outstanding examples of educational innovations. During his tenure, Pittsburgh was well known for its exemplary staff development programs.

In 1990, Dr. Wallace received the prestigious Harold W. McGraw, Jr. Prize in Education for restoring confidence in public education in Pittsburgh; he was the first superintendent of schools to receive this award. In 1992, the Council of the Great Cities Schools honored him with the Richard L. Green Award for contributions to urban education. In 1989, he was named Pennsylvania's Superintendent of the Year.

Dr. Wallace began his career as a teaching principal in rural Maine. He later held positions as principal, assistant superintendent, and superintendent in Massachusetts. He also spent 4 years as an administrator in educational research and development institutions. He received his BS degree from Gorham (Maine) State College and MEd and EdD from Boston College. He spent a year as a postdoctoral fellow at Stanford University.

To my wife, Rita,
and daughters Monica, Margaret, and Mona.

PART

I

Principles of Educational Leadership

CHAPTER

1

Prerequisites for Educational Leadership

The superintendent of education is expected to be a visionary leader. Guided by a clear vision of excellence, he or she organizes the human and financial resources of a school district to pursue excellence in the performance of students, professionals, and support personnel. He or she seeks commitments from the community's stakeholders to support an excellence agenda for the schools and, equally important, empowers the district's professionals to create, implement, and evaluate this agenda.

Excellence, Vision, and Visionary Leadership

The concepts of *excellence, vision,* and *visionary leadership* are central to the thesis of this book; therefore, they require definition and description.

What Is Excellence?

Excellence is referred to frequently in educational literature but not often defined. *Webster's Dictionary* (1993, p. 791) defines excellence as "the state of possessing good qualities in an eminent degree." To be understood fully in education, this needs to be translated from the abstract to what people actually do when engaging in what is labeled *excellence.*

What Is Vision?

Excellence in education is closely related to what we refer to as *vision.* Vision and visionary leadership are concepts common in the fields of business and management as well as in education.

In management, vision is understood as a mental image of the future state of an organization that we hope to create (Senge, 1990, p. 9); this definition applies to education as well. Vision also connotes the attributes of realism, credibility, and attractiveness (Nanus, 1992). A vision of the future state of a school district, therefore, would have to be a realistic, attainable goal for key stakeholders. Put into operation, the concepts of excellence and vision guide the content and processes of the desired future state of a school in its mission as a learning institution, imaging the best possible conditions for students to learn and for teachers to teach.

The *vision statement* created by a school or a school district is the basis for an action plan to develop and implement an agenda to put the vision of excellence into practice. The *excellence agenda* extends the vision statement by making explicit the goals that must be achieved for the vision to become a reality in schools. What the superintendent does to attain this reality is the essence of educational visionary leadership.

What Is Visionary Leadership?

An effective visionary leader is one who inspires workers within an organization, relates well to individuals outside the organization, sets the direction for his or her organization, and enables the organization to cope with change. The critical roles for a visionary leader to implement are those of *direction setter, change agent, spokesperson,* and *coach* (Nanus, 1992, p. 13).

The superintendent as visionary leader sets the direction for a school district by articulating a vision of excellence—the basis for a covenant of values to which all stakeholders can subscribe (Sergiovanni, 1992). As a change agent, he or she is the catalyst for implementing initiatives to bring about the shared vision; the superintendent must understand change processes and anticipate actions needed to achieve the excellence agenda. As spokesperson, the superintendent becomes the chief advocate for the district's agenda, both within the school district and in the community. He or she must articulate the agenda to various publics in ways that will be meaningful to them. Finally, as a coach, the superintendent empowers and guides the professionals under his or her aegis to create the conditions to implement the excellence agenda.

Building a Vision of Excellence

One good way to build a vision of educational excellence is to generate an idea of the type of school and classrooms where students and teachers engage in the most productive and exciting learning that you can imagine. Then, consider in greater detail what teachers would be saying and doing with students and what students would be doing on their own and with classmates to bring about these best possible learning procedures and outcomes. Going further, what kind of school climate would be necessary to allow students, teachers, and principals to be maximally productive? Then imagine the kind of central office structure and the board-superintendent relationships that would optimize the conditions for students, professionals, and support personnel to function at their best.

It should be noted that you are creating the most ideal state of excellence when you engage in this exercise. In all probability, you will be describing behaviors that do not necessarily correspond with reality. Achieving what you envision may require substantial behavior change on the part of each stakeholder. The purpose in imagining the most excellent state you can conceive of is to establish the ideal as a benchmark against which you can measure progress.

When you create this mental image, you have taken the first step toward developing your own personal vision of educational excellence on which you can build an excellence agenda. When you share your vision with others, you identify a common core of understanding to guide your collective pursuit toward excellence in education.

The next section of this chapter presents some specific ideas for constructing one's vision of educational excellence that are illustrative, not prescriptive. A covenant of shared values agreed on by the major stakeholders in a school district will result from a blending of many perspectives.

The Superintendent's Leadership
for Excellence Within the School District

The superintendent provides direct leadership to central office personnel and both direct and indirect leadership to principals and teachers. Central office personnel offer direct service to teachers and principals; teachers and principals, in turn, give direct service to students to achieve the excellence goals for schools.

In the superintendent's varying degrees of direct and indirect leadership, students are the major focus. They are the recipients of all the efforts of professionals striving to achieve excellence in education. The following scenarios for students, teachers, principals, central office personnel, and the superintendent illustrate their pursuits.

Excellence for Students

Envision students engaged in active, authentic learning experiences. Hands-on learning and problem-solving activities promote the acquisition of knowledge and skills. Authentic learning engages students in "hard work" to gain substantive knowledge (Newmann, 1992). In these environments, students often engage in cooperative learning activities that promote higher-order outcomes. Working together to solve problems, they learn skills related to planning, sharing workload, and other social interaction skills that prepare them to work in groups. Higher-order outcomes require them to understand and synthesize what they have learned in ways that can be generalized to other learning situations.

A caring environment is an important aspect of excellent learning milieus for students and is characterized by mutual respect and fairness among students and adults. It is also where high expectations are communicated for the performance of students, professionals, and support staff members.

Excellence for Teachers

Teachers engaged in authentic teaching ask questions that provoke student thinking. They engage students in the learning process by posing problematic situations for them to explore and ask questions that require them to seek relationships among and between information or sources of knowledge as opposed to asking for recall of information. Teachers expect students to come to conclusions about the meanings of materials that they have encountered. Authentic teaching requires that teachers engage students in sustained dialogue about matters of serious educational consequences (Newmann & Wehlage, 1993). In a classroom characterized by active, authentic learning, students do not sit passively for long periods of time listening to teachers telling them what they need to know, nor do teachers do the thinking for students.

Another perspective on excellent teaching emerges from 25 years of work in schools sponsored by the Ford Foundation (Academy for Educational Development, 1985). The concept of teacher development describes growth of skill from novice to the most mature and effective level of performance—differentiated pedagogy. Teachers who use differentiated pedagogy plan for each student in a class, based on a recognition of that learner's current state of knowledge and skill. Teachers functioning at this level of sophistication in instruction group students for short-term learning tasks; as students demonstrate mastery or the need for more practice, teachers regroup them appropriately. Such responsiveness to readiness level maximizes success for learners.

In addition to possessing high-quality pedagogical skills, teachers who promote excellence create an environment of care and concern through high interpersonal regard for their students. In a caring environment, all participants have high expectations for one another and strive to maintain consistency in relationships.

Excellence for Principals

As the superintendent is the educational leader for the school district and the community, the principal fills this role for the school, placing the educational welfare of his or her students as the top priority. Ideally, the principal

> creates an environment for teachers and students that optimizes learning;
>
> removes barriers to learning by protecting learning time for students;
>
> reviews the educational progress of students through careful analyses of grade reporting, standardized tests, and other indicators of students' progress;
>
> visits classrooms frequently to communicate interest in their welfare and progress to students and teachers; and
>
> observes and confers with teachers to improve the quality of instruction delivered to students.

The principal engages the staff members in creating a school's vision that merges with the district's, to create an excellence agenda for the school. The school vision reflects the unique characteristics of that school and the population it serves; it emerges from substantive discussion with faculty, parents, and others and results in the publication of a covenant of shared values. The principal is the chief advocate for the school, constantly promoting and gaining support for its vision and excellence agenda among faculty, students, parents, and the community.

The principal creates a supportive environment to promote professional growth for teachers and other certified personnel. Through individual conferences and faculty meetings, he or she initiates dialogue about professional improvement (see Chapters 5 and 10 for details on professional development of principals and teachers).

Above all, the principal creates a caring environment for students, professionals, staff members, and parents. He or she communicates respect for everyone by the manner in which he or she deals with children, youth, and adults, consciously creating a set of norms (characterized by caring and fairness) that govern the formal and informal structure of the school. In matters of discipline, the principal strives to maintain fairness and consistency. These conditions establish the foundation to build excellence in education at the school level.

Excellence for Central Office Personnel

The concept of excellent performance is relevant for all personnel engaged in providing support services. For example, central office staff members who provide support services must develop a vision of service excellence within their own areas of responsibility. They must reflect on the kind of service they provide and have high expectations for the quality of their performance. They must assume individual responsibility to maintain current knowledge regarding the trends and developments in their field through reading professional journals and attending local, regional, and national conferences.

For those central office people with major responsibility for support services and the supervision of others (e.g., supervisor of buildings and grounds), the goal of excellence requires that they work with assigned personnel to articulate how their particular service supports the vision of the district. Each support service must identify how it can contribute to the common good and the fulfillment of the vision. Central office personnel must realize that their primary purpose is to facilitate the effective operation of the schools. Constant vigilance about ways to improve the quality and efficiency of service to clients lays the foundation for excellence.

In dealing with district personnel, parents, and the general public, central office staff members are expected to treat everyone with respect and courtesy, mirroring the caring environment created in the schools. An atmosphere of excellence becomes the norm in an environment where respect for others is expected.

Excellence for the Superintendent

The superintendent is the central person responsible for achieving the excellence agenda of the school district whose ideal role encompasses the following:

- Combining and arranging the elements of visionary leadership to achieve the maximum positive outcomes for students
- Blending the elements of the district's agenda to achieve excellence in performance for all stakeholders
- Setting the tone for the district's personnel and the community by modeling the interpersonal regard that is expected of all the stakeholders
- Ensuring that the efforts of all stakeholders are synchronized
- Being the visible presence for the schools in the community, reminding all the stakeholders of the vision of excellence embraced by the district
- Confronting, with dignity, those professionals who are not reaching the level of performance required and taking appropriate action
- Anticipating and seeking out problems that emerge as the excellence agenda is being implemented
- Resolving problems through analysis, development of alternative solutions, and implementation of a strategy

The Superintendent's
Leadership Role Within the Community

The following sections describe the excellence that a superintendent seeks from the board, parents, and the community.

Excellence for the Board

The board of education contributes by specifically approving the excellence agenda and adopting policies and procedures that support it. An excellent board

> recognizes its fundamental role in establishing policy for the school district,
>
> charges the superintendent and the administration to develop plans to implement the vision and excellence agenda,
>
> approves the strategic plan and monitors the progress of its implementation with the superintendent,
>
> maintains a hands-off posture regarding the day-to-day operations of the school district,
>
> avoids patronage regarding personnel appointments or promotions, and
>
> holds administration to a high standard of performance relating to the policies and procedures designed to achieve the goals of the excellence agenda.

The board, through its president and officers,

> channels to the superintendent the concerns of parents and community—where appropriate, they ask the superintendent to take action;
>
> endorses the excellence agenda through formal vote;
>
> proactively advocates with parents and the community for the annual budget to ensure that sufficient funds are available to meet the goals;
>
> maintains harmonious and effective working relationships with the superintendent and each other;
>
> develops and maintains trust in communications with each other and the superintendent as well as with professional and support staff members, parents, and the general public;
>
> maintains the focus on their agenda by frequently reviewing progress and by visiting schools to see plans in action;
>
> takes appropriate action, recommended by the superintendent, to keep the excellence agenda on course;

maintains proper relationships with employees without showing favoritism to particular individuals or groups;

recognizes that board members are partners in progress with the professionals of the district, the parents, and the community; and assumes a statesmanship role as an advocate for excellence.

Excellence for Parents

Parents are the key stakeholders in an excellence agenda. The future of their children is at stake and requires them to become partners with school leaders, teachers, and the board. Ideally, parents who embrace the district's excellence agenda

recognize that they are their child's first teachers,

accept the responsibility to work with teachers and administrators to enhance the education of their children,

realize that they must create a supportive home environment to encourage their child's educational progress,

provide quiet time and help where needed to assist children in their homework and school projects, and

stay in close communication with the teachers of their children to ensure that adequate educational progress is made.

Excellent parents recognize when they need help in addressing the educational or social needs of their children and are willing to seek it from the schools or community agencies. Taylor's (1992) research, for example, indicates that parents want the same goals for their children whether they live in poverty or affluence; they want their children to be successful in school and in life. Some parents living in poverty, however, do not know how to effectively access schools or community agencies to receive help for their children. Principals, teachers, counselors, and social workers should assist parents in finding appropriate resources to help fulfill their dreams for their children.

Excellence for the Community

The general welfare of any community—rural, suburban, or urban— demands a high-quality education for children and youth. One cornerstone of a healthy community is an excellent school system that effectively meets the educational, social, and health needs of children, youth, and families.

A community that commits to achieving educational excellence recognizes two important concepts: (a) schools must prepare young people to participate effectively in the economic, social, and political life of the community as citizens; and (b) community agencies and institutions make a direct contribution to the attainment of educational excellence.

Building the Shared Vision for Excellence

Vision building is both an individual and a group enterprise. A common vision begins with the vision of each individual involved (Senge, 1990, p. 21). As mentioned earlier, the superintendent provides the leadership for the creation of and the agreement on a common vision at the district level. At the school level, the principal provides similar leadership. The process of a shared vision has two important elements: (a) It requires extensive dialogue between the key stakeholders to agree on a statement of beliefs about the desired future state of the school district and individual schools and (b) it requires each participant to think seriously about personal beliefs regarding knowledge, learning, teaching, assessment, and the like.

The final product of deliberations, the vision statement, communicates the beliefs of the stakeholders and the future state of affairs they seek to attain and represents a covenant of shared values (Sergiovanni, 1992). This covenant becomes (a) the living document that orients and directs the work of the professionals in the school district; (b) the statement of core values shared by the school, the district, and the community; (c) the vehicle by which to build an excellence agenda; (d) the foundation for the strategic plan that specifies the goals, objectives, activities, and expected outcomes for the agenda; and (e) the basis for the evaluative criteria by which judgments will be made about attainment of the excellence goals.

What Kind of Commitment Is Required?

Reaching the goals embodied in the vision statement and the excellence agenda requires that the superintendent make educational leadership his or her top priority. The principals must follow suit at the school level, and the board of education must make the excellence agenda its top priority, using it as the guiding principle for all district operations—educational and support.

Delegating Management Functions

A commitment to excellence requires that the superintendent organize central office staff members to assume major responsibility for the management of the school district. The superintendent must hold others fully accountable for the effective operation of the district's management affairs. Delegating managerial tasks does not absolve the superintendent of personal accountability for effective operations; it does mean that he or she will spend less time dealing directly with management details and more time overseeing and guiding educational issues. Through careful design of the organizational structure, appropriate delegation of responsibility, and effective reporting procedures, the superintendent can clear the daily calendar to be free to provide the educational leadership required to implement the district's vision and be the chief spokesperson to the stakeholders and the general public.

Exercising Educational Leadership Through Teams

The superintendent can and should build leadership teams to help implement the excellence agenda. To do this, the superintendent must

ensure that key personnel at the school and district levels understand the vision, the excellence agenda, and district's strategic implementation plan;

keep district personnel focused on the goals of the agenda by frequently referring to them and by reviewing its progress; and

visit schools and monitor activities to communicate the importance of the agenda as well as to encourage professionals and support personnel in their work.

The annual budgets for each school and the district become important vehicles. The budget becomes the fiscal counterpart of the educational plans to support and achieve the district's and the school's vision of excellence.

Achieving a Commitment to Excellence

This section focuses on the components needed to achieve a commitment to excellence. This process requires that the superintendent unite the board, build effective union relationships, pull together the professional staff members, gain the support of parents and the community, secure financial resources, and widely communicate the excellence agenda.

Uniting the Board of Education

With a board united in its resolve to support and achieve the excellence agenda, the goals can be met. The board must adopt the agenda through formal vote and support the plans and the budget to implement it. How can this be accomplished when many stakeholders other than the board will be involved?

First, the board establishes priorities that set the parameters for the vision and the excellence agenda. These priorities become the boundaries for planning and vision development by the stakeholder groups (see Chapter 3).

Second, once the vision statement and the agenda have evolved, the board must formally adopt them. This adoption demonstrates the commitment of the board. Maintaining the board's commitment requires that they be fully informed of the progress of the schools and the district toward meeting the goals of the agenda.

Building Effective Union Relations

To improve the quality of education in a school district, the leaders and members of both teacher and administrator unions need to be committed to the agenda. Support of the union leaders is absolutely critical, and the superintendent needs to meet with the union leadership prior to initiating any aspect of building the vision and the excellence agenda. Together, they must reach agreement about how the unions are to be involved in the process and the type of commitment that they must make. Engagement of these significant stakeholders will ultimately determine whether the agenda will be achieved.

Other unions that may not have direct involvement in the educational practices of the district, such as those for support services, also need to be informed of the strategic plans. They should be invited to engage in discussions about the vision so that they see themselves as part of the larger effort to achieve the excellence agenda for the school district. Involving these union personnel in identifying ways in which they can contribute to the excellence agenda promotes a concern for the general welfare of the district.

Uniting the Professional Staff to Support the Excellence Agenda

A new agenda for excellence can be very threatening to veteran teachers and administrators because it implies change. The expressed or implied need to learn new skills or content or do things in a different way can cause significant anxiety. Research on educational change provides us with an understanding of the personal and institutional dynamics that accompany new initiatives (Fullan & Stiegelbauer, 1991; Hall & Hord, 1987). The knowledge from this research can help superintendents and school principals address these issues constructively.

One significant way to unite the professional staff is to engage them in planning and creating the district's vision statement and excellence agenda. The superintendent must be careful to see that all levels of schooling are included in districtwide planning committees; proportional representation with respect to demographic variables, such as gender, race, ethnicity, age, experience in the district, and the like, is crucial to success.

Teachers and principals can sometimes become cynical about new educational initiatives, based on negative experiences with previous innovations; such experiences may cause problems in generating genuine interest in a new excellence agenda. The superintendent must convince professionals by actions and words that a serious commitment is being made. The strong actions of a board in adopting such an agenda and providing financial support to achieve it is the best communication of its seriousness of purpose. Most important, the professionals of the district will watch very carefully to see that the superintendent and the board are consistent in supporting the agenda and following through in its implementation.

Teachers will begin to believe when they perceive genuine, long-term follow-through by the superintendent, central office administrators, principals, and the board. The implementation of an excellence agenda will not succeed unless a climate of trust and mutual respect unites the teachers, administrators, superintendent, and the board.

Gaining Support of Parents and Community

Parents and community leaders will support the excellence agenda to the extent that they are involved in its development. Key parent and community leaders can be directly involved in developing the vision statements through membership on planning or steering committees at the district or the school level. The broader community can be involved in the development of the district's vision by participation in public forums, which provide opportunities for residents who do not have children in school to provide input.

Securing Financial Support

In all probability, a substantial amount of the cost of the excellence agenda will be for professional development. The board needs to be prepared to set aside a minimum of at least 1% of its total budget for professional development activities (see Chapter 5 for details). The professional development plan and budget will reflect a specific sequence of activities based on the comprehensive nature of the skill or knowledge development required.

The superintendent should develop a formal plan to seek funding from the state education agency and federal agencies to augment local funding. It is typical for state educational agencies to have discretionary funding available for projects related to specific priorities. The superintendent and associated staff members should be aggressive in seeking sources of funding to support the excellence agenda by aligning district plans with state priorities when appropriate.

In the past, federal agencies have had some funding for national educational priorities. At this point, the level of future federal support for education is unclear. The superintendent, however, should have the *Federal Register* and other relevant publications reviewed for funding possibilities.

Local businesses also have a stake in the excellence agenda; an excellent school system is the foundation for a viable community. Business and industry understand that their future well-being depends on an educated workforce. More than ever before in the 20th century, business and industry recognize that an educated and educable workforce will be necessary for economic survival, and they recognize that the future workforce must be drawn from the growing populations of ethnic and racial minority groups. The emerging demographics of the nation make this fact very clear. The student population that the schools have typically not served well (poor and minority students) will be the mainstay of the future economy. The effective education of poor and minority students must become a joint goal of business and education.

Superintendents can capitalize on the interests and concerns of business and industry and forge relationships that will help secure financial support. Because the stakes in the economy are high, business people are more willing than ever to find ways to collaborate to improve the quality of high school graduates' education. Many businesses will be willing to provide funding or contribute personnel to help achieve specific goals that are consistent with their mission. The school district and local businesses must develop mutual trust if sharing of resources is to occur.

During the last quarter of the 20th century, business has been very critical of public education. Although the climate is now more favorable for cooperation, business enterprises want visible results from their investments of dollars or contributed personnel. If school districts want the support of the business community, they will have to accept a results-oriented posture and be willing to assume accountability for student learning.

In many communities, there are individual, family, or corporate philanthropic institutions. Many of these institutions have not supported public education. Through the efforts of public education funds, however, private and corporate financial support is now more readily available. A superintendent may work independently or with a public education fund to seek external resources for the excellence agenda. This activity should be viewed as part of the public relations campaign to promote the district's agenda. It also provides an opportunity to build the trusting relationships with key leaders that are so critical to successful community relations.

The contact with business and industrial leaders helps build general support for the school district's annual budget. By informing the community leadership of the excellence agenda, the superintendent can promote the goals of the school district and develop an understanding of its financial needs.

Communicating the Excellence Agenda

A comprehensive public information program will help develop support. Effective communications include the following:

- Brief news releases for the print and electronic media, geared to building public understanding of and commitment to the excellence agenda
- Brief informative announcements to district employees regarding the procedures being used to develop, and the progress being made in implementing, the agenda
- Public meetings that focus on part-to-whole relationships of the complex process of developing and implementing an excellence agenda

- Publications that incorporate a visual representation of the relationship of specific activities to the broader agenda
- Human interest stories designed to sustain media and public attention on the accomplishments of the district's goals
- Reports of interviews with students, teachers, administrators, and parents to help communicate the meaning of the excellence agenda

There will be many problems encountered in developing and implementing an excellence agenda. This chapter has presented an ideal state of excellence to which a superintendent might aspire. The real task of the superintendent is to exercise the leadership to identify and solve problems that will be found on the way to achieving the goals of excellence. Part II, Chapters 7 through 11, contains examples of what school districts have done to implement excellence agendas.

SUMMARY

This chapter has outlined the role of the superintendent as an educational leader; it presented the concepts of excellence, vision, visionary leadership, and an educational excellence agenda. Suggestions were presented regarding how all stakeholders might engage in developing the excellence agenda. Ideas were put forward to help superintendents maintain a focus on the agenda and to unite the stakeholder groups. Finally, thoughts were offered regarding the engagement of the business community, state and federal agencies, and private philanthropic groups to financially support the agenda.

The reality is that excellence in education must be achieved if public education is to survive. All stakeholders have a responsibility to contribute and commit to an excellence agenda for their communities' schools. The quality of life in the community requires it. Our promise to future generations demands it. The survival of our nation as a leading world economic power depends on it. Let's do it!

2

The Superintendent
as Educational Leader

The title "superintendent of education" connotes the emphasis of this book, placing the responsibility for educational matters first. The title "superintendent of schools," in contrast, tends to communicate an emphasis on managerial matters—buses, budgets, buildings, and bonds. I do not mean to denigrate the title of superintendent of schools; rather, I emphasize the superintendent's role with respect to education.

Educational Leadership

When superintendents make education the top priority for their leadership, they allocate their time to targeted tasks and delegate responsibility for management to competent subordinates. They still maintain accountability for the entire functioning of the school district, however. Ideally, the superintendent of education spends most administrative time monitoring and reviewing the work of the managerial staff. Later sections in this chapter deal with the processes of delegating and monitoring the work of managerial staff.

What Is an Educational Leader?

An educational leader is one who conceives of his or her role as concerned primarily with educational processes and outcomes. The superintendent as educational leader places primary emphasis on effective student learning and the creation of a supportive environment for the professional growth of teachers and administrators.

An educational leader engages in lifelong learning to expand his or her knowledge of trends in areas such as learning, learning theory, curricula and instructional practices, and the assessment of learning. One keeps abreast through professional reading and attending local, state, and national conferences on pertinent issues. An educational leader maintains close contact with supervisory personnel and outstanding teachers in the district to update his or her knowledge of current classroom practices.

How Does One Exercise Educational Leadership?

As stated in Chapter 1, educational leadership begins with the formulation of a personal vision of education for the common good. To provide effective leadership, a superintendent needs a clear conception of the desired ends sought and a well-defined set of means to achieve them. A personal vision is the crucial beginning point; only then can one lead others to develop a common vision. A district vision must evolve, through the exercise of leadership by the superintendent, to become one shared by all stakeholders.

My personal experience in dealing with the articulation of a vision and an excellence agenda is that constant repetition is required. Not all stakeholders are able to hold the big picture. The implementation of a strategic plan requires that certain activities occur as prerequisite to others. When beginning a 5-year plan, for example, some stakeholders—particularly classroom teachers, because of their relative isolation from one another—may not be able to "see the forest for the trees."

The superintendent and building administrators are responsible for helping the participants to perceive part-whole relationships; they need to assist classroom teachers to see the relationship between what they are doing and what is proposed. Maintaining a sense of continuity in educational experiences and teaching strategies is important to teachers. Providing for continuity and maintaining integration are major challenges for the superintendent and the principals.

Vision implementation through an excellence agenda requires the development of both a long-range strategic plan and an annual action plan. The long-range strategic plan sets the course for a school or a school district for a period of up to 5 years. The annual plan lays out the activities and goals to be achieved by the end of a given school year.

The superintendent must pay close attention to the implementation of annual plans for the district and for individual schools. Monitoring their implementation gives the superintendent a sense of the pulse of the district and lets him or her know when to intervene to keep the excellence agenda moving forward.

Effective educational leadership requires that the superintendent gather both qualitative and quantitative data for making decisions about program activities and outcomes. Formative evaluation is called for to identify potential changes in strategies or allocation of resources to maximize goal achievements.

When designing and implementing a strategic or annual plan, the focus should be on a limited number of initiatives and outcomes. Stakeholders may lose sight of the comprehensive plan if they are engaged in too many activities simultaneously. The superintendent should maintain focus for professionals, the board, parents, and the general public. The use of graphics in district publications helps stakeholders visualize overall goals and specific initiatives and can also be helpful in keeping the focus on short-term and long-range goals.

There is no substitute for constant reinforcement of a vision and an excellence agenda; it is critical to successful educational leadership. As previously stated, the superintendent bears the major responsibility for the articulation of the vision to the stakeholders and the general public.

What Does It Mean to Commit to Educational Leadership?

What does it really mean to make a commitment to be an educational leader? As a superintendent, it means that you communicate these values through the following words and actions.

First, allocate time to giving top priority in daily planning to educational matters; delegate day-to-day decisions for the operation of the district to responsible administrators and hold them accountable.

Second, recognize that you have to become a visible presence in the schools. When the superintendent takes the time out of his or her busy schedule to visit with teachers and communicate an interest in the progress and the problems of implementing the excellence agenda, it makes a strong statement!

Third, meeting frequently with task forces engaged in planning or implementing the agenda communicates interest and commitment to program development and evaluation.

I often viewed part of my work as superintendent as being a talent scout. The more opportunities I had to visit classrooms and meet with school faculty or task force members, the greater the chance of spotting potential leaders. Then, as opportunities arose, I would give these people an opportunity to demonstrate their skills; I would send them to conferences or engage them in activities to communicate my interest in their professional development. Also, when other school districts expressed an interest in our programs, I would send teachers or principals to talk to their peers. Having them disseminate information about district programs has the following multiple benefits:

- It communicates respect to teachers and principals and makes them feel an important part of the district's educational agenda.
- It increases their personal and professional confidence.
- It makes them feel fortunate to be part of a district on the move.

Fourth, participate with teachers and administrators in staff development training. This gives you firsthand knowledge about training quality and demonstrates to teachers and principals that "if it's good enough for you, it's got to be good enough for them."

I can't say enough about how important it is to participate with professionals as a learner. Among other things, it demonstrates that learning is a lifelong endeavor and a top priority for a superintendent. More important, perhaps, it tends to build camaraderie with the district's professional community. Maintaining your position as educational leader, you communicate that you are striving to become a better one. Thus, you model for your subordinates the type of behavior you expect of them.

Fifth, maintain focus by keeping the big picture in mind while moving the excellence agenda forward. Help others to focus on short-term goals while reminding them of the long-term ones. Continually articulate the vision and the excellence agenda. Sometimes it means developing a slogan to remind all stakeholders where the district is headed.

Obviously, to commit to a role as educational leader means that you have to believe in it and work at it. By placing education first, you define all other activities of the superintendent as supporting that main goal.

Using Data to Guide Educational Leadership

An important function of an educational leader is to carefully monitor the implementation of the excellence agenda, which requires the collection and analysis of a wide variety of both qualitative and quantitative data.

Documentation of major initiatives—records of implemented innovations—is a useful source of qualitative data. This includes reports of key meetings and events, items discussed, decisions made and not made, and other important incidents shaping the implementation of the excellence agenda. Other qualitative data may emerge from informal interviews with teachers, administrators, parents, and other stakeholders that provide descriptions of the context of implementation. Structured interviews with stakeholder groups can provide information about the status of implementation at specific points in time.

Quantitative data can be aggregated to provide a statistical picture of accomplishments. Survey data provide good quantitative information to complement structured interviews and can include the impressions of the stakeholders as they experience implementation of the excellence agenda. Surveys of teachers, administrators, parents, and students provide valuable information about classrooms that can be used to judge the success of implementation; they also help to identify potential or actual trouble spots in moving the agenda forward.

Using Data to Monitor Key School District Indicators

To verify the climate or the effectiveness of a school or district requires the constant monitoring of data that have a bearing on educational outcomes. It is also important to oversee carefully the management efficiency of the district as it affects general operations and support for educational initiatives.

Data useful in determining a district's progress include indices that track educational outcomes and processes. Unfortunately, there is a tendency to rely on the single indicator of standardized achievement test scores, which typically measure limited knowledge and skills of students and low levels of cognitive ability. Although it is difficult and costly for a district to develop more relevant indicators of educational progress, the effort should be made. Participating in activities such as the New Standards Project (Simmons & Resnick, 1993) gives the superintendent the opportunity to exercise leadership in the assessment of student learning.

Often, high school students' aggregate performance on the Scholastic Achievement Test (SAT) is used almost exclusively to judge the quality of a district's secondary education, but scores on the SAT are not achievement scores; they are indicators used to predict a student's likely performance as a college freshman. Equally important in judging the quality of educational outcomes are high school completion rates, postsecondary acceptance rates, student attendance, teacher attendance, and special achievements of students. The morale of schools and the district may be a strong factor in influencing educational outcomes. These sources of information are often overlooked in making judgments about the quality of education.

More often than not, school districts (as well as state and federal agencies) gather much more data than they effectively use. Often, important data are not analyzed, yet they and the relationships between them can have a great bearing on the health or effectiveness of a district. For example, analyzing the effectiveness of support services and intervening to solve problems improve the quality of service and boost the morale of teachers and principals. The superintendent needs to monitor financial expenditures and revenues. It is helpful, for example, to have parameters of anticipated expenditures and revenue to serve as early warning systems.

It is important to review data from a variety of educational, personnel, and financial sources to detect trends in the district. As a superintendent develops a keen sense for data that inform him or her about the status of the school district, he or she is able to provide more effective educational and managerial leadership.

Using Data to Make Program Decisions

Decisions regarding the continuation, modification, or termination of educational programs require comprehensive analysis and need more than one data set (e.g., student performance on a standardized test). Rather, a broad view of the effect of the innovation should be gathered through formal and informal surveys and structured interviews with pupils, teachers, principals, and parents. Data should be gathered by using the most applicable, valid, and reliable instruments available.

Most programs need some modification—some fine tuning to be sure that they are as effective as possible in producing positive results for students. Decisions to terminate a program should be based on as broad a data set as possible, including financial and educational data. Superintendents and boards need to be careful not to jump to conclusions about specific programs and make a decision to terminate without looking carefully at all the data. Programs are sometimes terminated because they are not cost-effective; sometimes, because they are not favorably perceived by any of the key stakeholder groups. Most often, however, programs are stopped because they just don't produce the intended results. Unless there are good reasons for making a precipitous decision, termination of a program should follow a deliberate process of data gathering and analysis so that the choice is an informed one.

Throughout my 19 years as a superintendent, I practiced a data orientation to educational leadership (Wallace, 1985b). I believe that data analysis provides the basis for clear definition of educational problems; I also believe that careful analysis of a problem generates potential solutions in the mind of the discerning observer. For example, an item analysis of standardized test scores can provide a detailed profile of strengths and weaknesses of students, grade levels within schools, and schools themselves. After such an analysis, program enhancements can be implemented to maximize strengths and minimize weaknesses. Climate surveys of individual schools can help identify organizational or communication problems. If the superintendent takes a facilitative, rather than a judgmental, approach to school climate data, actions can be taken at the school level to improve the quality of life for everyone involved.

Delegating Managerial Responsibility

The superintendent's first necessary step is to delegate the day-to-day operations of the district to competent subordinates. If these staff members are not accustomed to making decisions on their own, the superintendent will have to make it explicitly clear that he or she expects them to exercise their administrative judgment. If the superintendent comes to a district from the outside, it is important to set this expectation clearly from the first day. If appointed from inside the district, it is equally important for him or her to clarify expectations for those who may have been accustomed to a different modus operandi with the previous superintendent.

Communicating expectations is best done through a clear job description and evaluative criteria. Job descriptions for central office administrators should clearly state expectations regarding exercise of discretionary authority; the evaluative criteria need to reflect explicitly the outcomes for which they will be held accountable.

Reorganizing the central administration may be necessary to ensure that adequate resources—human and otherwise— are used where needed.

It may be necessary to add a position to facilitate planning and implementation. In my case, I created the position of planning coordinator; this person worked with me and with task forces to oversee the plans, budget estimations, and implementation schedules addressing the reform agenda. The planning coordinator reported to me and had the authority to work with constituent groups to develop the excellence agenda; the coordinator also prepared all action items required to implement it.

Delegating responsibility and accountability to central office administrators may require a cabinet structure, which provides the superintendent with frequent contact with key administrators to ensure that the district operates effectively and efficiently. The cabinet is made up of key officials of the district (e.g., assistant superintendents, business managers, personnel officers). The cabinet meets as frequently as needed to keep the superintendent abreast of events in the district.

In a large district, the superintendent may need to meet weekly with a subcabinet. I found it helpful to have key administrators submit weekly one-page summaries of the issues that they dealt with on a daily basis. These weekly reports gave me a sense of what was going on in the district and alerted me to potential problems that might need my attention. Such mechanisms can keep a superintendent informed about management activities, enabling him or her to focus on educational leadership.

In addition to explicit job descriptions, all central office administrators need annual goals. These goals, reviewed and approved by the superintendent or other appropriate person, keep administrators focused on accomplishments. For each area specified, the administrator needs to indicate how the goal will be achieved and criteria to verify its attainment. The job description, annual goals, and evaluative criteria together communicate expectations to staff members, which ensures that delegated responsibilities will be fulfilled.

Involving Participants in Planning

A key responsibility for the superintendent as educational leader is to build support for the excellence agenda. The best way to do that is to involve key stakeholders in the planning process right from the beginning. Chapter 3 describes a model for involvement of district and community representatives in the development of priorities and plans.

Rallying Community Support

Following the board's adoption of the excellence agenda, the superintendent can exercise leadership by scheduling a press conference to announce the agenda and describe it in detail. He or she should also schedule visits with the editorial staff of print and electronic media for these significant people to learn firsthand about the agenda and establish the foundation for editorial comment and follow-up stories. Such meetings allow the media to broaden their understanding of the goals and specific strategies of the excellence agenda. One-time visits with media executives are not enough, however; annual meetings should be scheduled to bring them up to date on the progress being made and to further their knowledge of the agenda. Time spent in this way will pay significant dividends in establishing and maintaining a positive relationship with the local media, which predisposes them to be more positive and constructive in handling the day-to-day news of the school district.

Superintendents in large districts quickly become aware that good news about the school district is not always seen as news in the media. A cursory view of headlines and lead stories on television and radio quickly confirms that bad news makes headlines and consumes an inordinate share of ink and broadcast time. Getting the good news out about the district's pursuit of an excellence agenda often requires some human interest story. By maintaining open lines of communication and being honest with the media, the superintendent sets the stage for good media relations and increases the likelihood that good news stories will be used (Wallace, 1990).

The superintendent should take every opportunity to address service groups, community associations, church groups, and local parent-teacher associations. Keeping state and federal legislators informed about the excellence agenda is also important so that they can talk knowledgeably with their constituents about the school district. Also, keeping in contact with legislators will help when you seek additional funding from the state or federal government.

Local government officials need know about the excellence agenda. Local government structure will dictate its interface with the school district. Where local government officials have direct influence on the school district (e.g., approval of the annual budget), it is critically important to maintain open communication. Where the legal relationship is indirect (e.g., the district is politically and fiscally independent), it is still important to maintain good working relationships. Informed government officials tend to be more positively disposed toward the school district. If government officials tend toward the negative, keeping them up to date and responding to their concerns may modify their views.

Being Visible in the Schools

Support for the educational agenda is enhanced when the superintendent visits schools and communicates that he or she is knowledgeable about educational trends and initiatives. An educational leader also offers advice, direction, and support for initiatives during school visits. A superintendent provides leadership for excellence by communicating directly to teachers and students in classrooms, thus affirming their efforts and progress.

Being visible requires that the superintendent periodically attend faculty meetings or participate in districtwide faculty assemblies. At these meetings, the superintendent continues to articulate the priorities of the district, the shared vision for educational excellence, and progress achieved. These meetings provide firsthand information regarding the faculty's perception and reception of the excellence agenda and provide teachers with an opportunity to get to know the superintendent. Such interactions confirm the vision and highlight the faculty's role in implementation.

Firsthand observation in the classroom provides the superintendent with direct student contact and the opportunity to garner their perceptions about the district and the programs being implemented. By asking questions and listening to students' answers, the superintendent communicates interest in their welfare and progress. In meetings with student government members, the superintendent listens to their perceptions about new initiatives and ways in which they believe the schools could be improved.

When meeting with student groups, it is wise for the superintendent to make it explicitly clear that discussion of problems in schools is to be of a general nature; in addition, students' comments must be made without specific reference to the names of individual teachers or administrators. This admonition assures teachers and administrators that students are not being used to evaluate the school's personnel. Students, as the primary clients and consumers of the excellence agenda, provide useful information to the superintendent. Like other data collected for formative evaluation purposes, information from students needs to be weighed together with the data collected from all sources.

Students can be very helpful in identifying aspects of school life that affirm or negate the sense of care, interest, and respect demonstrated by adults. Firestone, Rosenblum, and Webb (1987) indicate that students will commit themselves to school and to learning to the extent that adults in the schools communicate care and respect for them as individuals, treat students fairly, engage them actively in the learning process, and show the relationship between what they are learning and the work world.

Informal data gathered during school visits combined with other data (e.g., student dropout rates) can help the superintendent identify conditions that can and should be improved in the schools.

SUMMARY

The superintendent of education affirms the educational leadership role by placing education first on the daily agenda. He or she leads the district in the development of a shared vision, an excellence agenda, and a strategic plan to implement it. By being a visible presence in the schools, the superintendent (a) communicates support for the excellence agenda to teachers and administrators, (b) gathers informal data to help identify where interventions can more effectively implement the agenda, (c) confirms its importance to students, and (d) articulates the vision and the agenda for the school district to key stakeholders.

To exercise active educational leadership, the superintendent must delegate the general operations of the district to competent subordinates. This does not absolve the superintendent of accountability. Effective delegation is more easily achieved in an efficient organization that has explicit job expectations and annual goals for central office administrators.

The superintendent must also be the educational leader for the community. As such, the superintendent must keep parents, the general public, the media, and governmental leaders informed of the progress of the school district.

The superintendent uses data to guide him or her in making decisions to modify, expand, or terminate programs and to confirm the attainment of the excellence agenda.

3

Getting Started
With a Needs Assessment

An old Chinese proverb states that a long journey begins with the first step. The development and implementation of an excellence agenda will be a long journey. The first step is to determine where you are, gathering information to verify and clarify the current status of the district, and to establish benchmarks to measure future progress. Among the records that should be collected and analyzed are student achievement, student attendance, professional attendance, and the like. Financial data that provide costs per pupil for instruction, special programs, and cost trends over the past 5 years will also help to describe the status quo.

The second step on the journey to excellence is developing a clear sense of direction and destination. The end point you seek is expressed in the goals of the overall effort—the excellence agenda. The direction is expressed in a strategic plan detailing actions to reach the goals. One good way to begin is to conduct a needs assessment of the district. The next sections deal with the concept of a needs assessment and how to implement such a study.

Assessing the Needs of the District

A *need* is a condition that can or should be improved. There are two specific reasons for assessing the needs of a district: (a) to determine the extent to which the district is meeting the educational needs of children and youth and (b) to gather data that suggest priorities for improvement. According to Cooley and Bickel (1986), a needs assessment is designed to identify conditions in a school district that can and should be improved to ensure sound educational programs.

The primary assumption underlying a needs assessment is that the process and the results will help the district understand more fully where it is at the time of assessment. A secondary assumption is that the process will reveal a rather clear picture of what improvements need to be made to reach the goals espoused by the key stakeholders. Implicitly or explicitly, stakeholders describe a desired future state of affairs as they identify conditions that need to be improved. For example, in the 1980 needs assessment conducted in Pittsburgh, all stakeholder groups identified personnel evaluation as an imperative need of the district. Part of the survey included open-ended items to elicit additional information. Respondents suggested that (a) clear job descriptions be developed for all professionals and (b) professionals be held accountable for performing tasks specified in the job description. This is only one example of specific recommendations that emerged from this 1980 survey.

Organizing Existing Data for Analysis

Educators and educational agencies collect enormous amounts of data but seldom take the time to analyze or use them for improvement. For example, school districts gather information about student suspensions, class size, enrollment, and attendance patterns, but they do not often analyze these data to see if relationships exist between them. Secondary school administrators frequently do not examine the relationships between grade distributions, student attendance, class cuts, referrals to the office, and teacher attendance, yet an analysis of these data can be revealing in terms of the effects of teachers and teaching style on students and their achievement. To fully describe its current status, school districts should collect and analyze student data, school information, and financial data. Analysis of data by school, grade, gender, and race is often useful. Information that is useful to describe a district's status includes but is not limited to the following considerations:

- Percentage of retention
- Percentage of attendance
- Percentage of students in special education, Chapter I programs, or bilingual programs
- Percentage of out-of-school suspensions and reasons for them
- Percentage of students scoring at or above national norms on standardized tests on various subjects
- Percentage of students who participate in interscholastic academic competitions (debate, science fairs, etc.)

Other useful data include, but are not limited to, the following:

- Percentage of school completion rate by school (cohort survival)
- Class size by school, grade level, and subject (middle and secondary levels)
- Circulation of library books per student per year
- School climate survey data
- Cost per pupil, by school and subject, for electives at middle and secondary levels
- Comparative financial information for similar school districts

Planning for the Collection of New Data

Analysis of existing data and the determination of the relationships between them set the stage for the identification of any needed new information. Existing data provide a description of the status quo, whereas the collection and analysis of new information will provide a glimpse of the desired future. Planning for the collection of new data begins with a review of these questions:

Who are the decision makers?

What decisions are they going to make?

In what form do they want information to assist them in the decision-making process?

When do they want the information?

In a district needs assessment survey, the answers to these questions establish the framework for the data gathering. The decision makers will be the board of education; they will set priorities for the district. The board will need information from the district's key stakeholders about conditions that should be improved to make the schools more effective. The data will need to be given to the board in time to influence the development of the next budget.

Once these questions have been answered, planning for the survey can proceed. The collection of new data begins with the identification of areas to explore and the population to be sampled. Stakeholder groups should be identified who can provide the information to help determine the priority needs of the district. They need to be interviewed or surveyed to gather their ideas for improvement of the district. The following sections describe the development of surveys to gather the needed data.

Getting Started on the Needs Assessment

The superintendent has the responsibility for organizing the needs assessment survey. A good place to begin is to identify a group of professionals and community members to serve as advisers. The advisory committee assists in planning and overseeing the needs assessment survey; this group should be made up of representatives from the following:

Professional and support service groups within the district

Parents

Community leaders representing the various constituent groups served by the school district

Representatives of local government, social agencies, and service agencies

Other groups with whom school personnel come in frequent contact

Finally, the evaluation experts who will actually develop the surveys, collect and analyze the data, and prepare the drafts of the report are also working members of the committee. Personnel from outside the district (e.g., a university, a consulting firm) should be engaged if the district does not have its own skilled evaluation staff. These specialists need to understand that their role is one of serving the client, namely, the superintendent and the needs assessment advisory committee (Cooley & Bickel, 1986).

The advisory committee members serve three important functions. First, as opinion leaders, they represent their group and disseminate the first wave of information to their peers. Second, they are an important source of information in identifying the key issues facing the district, seen from their particular perspectives, from which come the items for the survey protocols and instruments. Third, they advise the superintendent regarding the needs assessment and thus build and maintain some degree of ownership of the data to be collected and the processes by which they will be collected, organized, and reported.

An important task for this advisory committee is to identify other groups who need to contribute data to the survey but who are not represented on the committee. For example, parents of children who attend private or parochial schools may provide some important perceptions of public education even though they do not participate in the system.

Another task is brainstorming to identify issues around which to design the survey; brainstorming helps identify the conditions or issues that must be addressed so the school district can become more effective and more efficient. Tentatively agreed-on major themes can serve as the basis for evaluation specialists to meet with other groups (e.g., teachers). The specialists can then solicit issues to frame the content of the survey and recommend the different instruments to be used. Following the brainstorming sessions and identification of target populations, the evaluation specialists can develop survey instruments and protocols for review by the superintendent and the advisory committee.

As stated earlier, this committee serves as an advisory group to the superintendent. The superintendent needs to remind them of their proper, yet important, role as advisers; it needs to be made clear from the outset that the superintendent is the final decision maker. Advisory groups sometimes have a tendency to view themselves as decision-making groups.

Developing the Survey Instruments

The development of survey instruments begins by interviewing a representative sample of each group to be surveyed, using the issues identified by the advisory group as the basis for these interviews. Interviews provide detailed information about how each group perceives the issues. Evaluators can capture the nuances of language that stakeholder groups use to talk about the issues; this language can then be used to develop items for the survey or protocols for structured interviews. From the data collected, evaluators can build survey items and organize them into draft instruments. The number of different instruments to be used is a judgment call made by the superintendent in consultation with the evaluators. It may be necessary, for example, to develop a different survey for central office or supervisory personnel compared with teachers, because of their different perspectives.

The instruments and protocols for structured interviews are then pilot tested with a small sample of each group to judge the efficacy of the items. A debriefing held with some members of each group provides insights about how they responded to particular items and the total survey; this information can be useful in preparing the final instruments. After any necessary revisions, the survey instruments and interview protocols are given to the advisory committee for their reactions.

In designing surveys, keep in mind that most instruments are administered to a sampling of professional groups and parents. A representative sample of some groups is most efficiently obtained by telephone. In the case of board members and key community leaders, it is best to conduct personal interviews using a structured interview protocol. With some populations, such as principals, it is wise to administer survey instruments to all members. With large groups, a 10% random sampling may provide sufficient data to make valid inferences. With senior citizens, it is probably best to conduct interviews in person; if this is not possible, telephone interviews are a good alternative. With student groups, it is most useful to conduct focus group meetings using a structured discussion format. Gathering data in these manners generally provides the most useful information in helping to identify the conditions in the school district that can and should be improved.

A technique to enrich survey results is to include open-ended questions that provide respondents opportunities for written comments. Often, this provides a rich source of contextual information that can be used to personalize the survey findings. Another important device is to ask respondents to rank order the three to five most important items in a particular section or category of the survey. This gives the evaluators a sense of those items most important to the respondents.

Once the decision is made to go ahead with the survey instruments, the schedules for administration, data collection, analysis, and presentation must be finalized. Then, the real work begins.

Organizing the Data for Presentation

As evaluation specialists organize the data for presentation, they need to review the decision questions listed on page 33 to clarify the purpose for which the information will be used. For busy decision makers (e.g., board members), the information needs to be presented in a way that is useful for setting priorities for the district. For professional groups and other stakeholders, the information needs to "tell a story" about the perceptions of those surveyed and the implications for school improvement.

Although the data used for decision making and public information are essentially the same, they may need to be organized and presented differently. Board members, who will use the data to set priorities, will need full sets of data and the time to analyze them and explore relationships. The board will need a full day to receive reports and interact with the evaluators and the superintendent before coming to some tentative agreement about setting priorities. On the other hand, teachers, administrators, and the general public need to be briefed on the salient findings of the survey; these briefings should last about 1 hour. The media will report on only the highlights and thus will need summaries to make their reporting process easy; however, the media should have access to the complete data if they wish.

The superintendent and the evaluators need to plan the presentation of the information to the board carefully. The evaluators, as a result of individual interviews with board members, will have a sense of what is of concern to them. The superintendent, because of frequent dealing with the board, will have insights about how information should be presented. The presentation should begin with a review of the data that describes the status quo of the district.

Board members may be familiar with much of the data in general because they deal with educational issues on a monthly basis. They may not, however, have had the opportunity to examine relationships between the data that may identify some real opportunities for improvement in the district. Board members will have some knowledge about standardized test scores; they may not have reviewed item analyses of these data that would show particular strengths or weaknesses of the district. The presentation to the board should highlight those findings that both explain current conditions and imply specific corrective actions.

The board needs a presentation of the needs assessment data that highlights findings in common across population subgroups. For instance, if all populations report the need to improve personnel evaluation, this finding needs to be forcefully presented to the board. The main focus, then, should be on those areas of broad consensus among all of the stakeholders. If, for example, the majority of the stakeholder groups identify a need for making decisions at the school level, this needs to be highlighted. A second emphasis in the board's presentation should be on findings of specific groups. The board needs to understand how each of the stakeholder groups perceives the issues and the conditions that could and should be improved.

After the superintendent and the evaluators have come to agreement on the presentation of the data to the board and to other groups, a dry run should be made to the board president. The purpose of this preview is to assess the effectiveness of the presentation. The presentation to the board should take place at a retreat site away from the regular meeting place. A retreat format, which engages the board in a seminar-type activity, allows for an informal dialogue with the evaluators and the superintendent and serves as a learning experience for the board. It provides ample opportunity to discuss issues and explore the meaning of data before identifying priorities and taking a formal vote in public session.

Immediately following the presentation to the board, several meetings should be scheduled for stakeholders. The data must be presented to the following groups: the needs assessment advisory committee, professional staff, support personnel, parents, students, and the general public. It is important for the professional staff to hear the results of the survey before the media receive them. News releases need to be prepared and a press conference needs to be scheduled.

Depending on the size of the district, briefings may need to be scheduled in several geographic areas for two important reasons: (a) to ensure the broadest possible dissemination of the findings and (b) to prepare the general public for the priorities that will be formally voted by the board. These important briefings lay the foundation for the involvement of the stakeholders in the subsequent development of a vision of educational excellence for the district.

Data-Based Priority Setting

A primary purpose of the needs assessment is to provide the board with a solid understanding of the key stakeholders' perceptions regarding the district's current status. Following the review of the data, the superintendent guides the board to prioritize the district's needs based on their own and others' perceptions. The superintendent leads the board to develop consensus on five or six major priority issues to be addressed. The board will vote on these priorities at the next public meeting. By affirming the priorities as the focus for planning, the board takes its first step in committing to the excellence agenda described in Chapter 2. The priorities become the parameters that guide the superintendent and the stakeholders to create a vision for the district and to subsequently develop and implement the agenda.

Prioritizing and rank ordering needs or issues will focus the efforts of the superintendent and key stakeholders on those conditions that deserve the most attention. Rank-ordered issues will be the focus for the subsequent development of the district's vision and the agenda for excellence. Not all problems can be addressed simultaneously. Some problems are easily addressed whereas others will require long-range strategies. Finally, the superintendent and staff can handle only a limited number of issues effectively.

Creating the Vision

Chapter 2 provided a definition of vision and highlighted its centrality to the school improvement process. Some important questions to ask include the following:

- How does the setting of priorities by the board influence the vision-building process?
- What are the relationships between the priorities, the vision statement, the excellence agenda, and the strategic plan?

The priorities established are the sine qua non for the vision statement. The vision for the district and subsequently for each school must, at a minimum, address the priorities. For example, let's assume that one of the board's priorities is to increase the quality of science education at all levels in the district. The vision statements for the district and for each school should reflect this priority. The board members have declared that science education is important; the board expects that groups involved in vision development will include this priority in the evolution of their vision statement. The statement of the board does not limit the creativity of the respective groups as they build their vision for the district or the schools— they are free to go far beyond the priorities in creating the image of the schools of the future for the district—but in doing so, they must address the issue of science education.

Priorities in and of themselves do not constitute a vision statement. Priorities tend to be specific; a vision statement is general. In the example stated earlier, the board identifies science education as a top priority for the district. The vision statement reflecting this priority would include a phrase such as "our students will be scientifically literate." Then, the subsequent excellence agenda will state the specific learning goals to enable students to achieve scientific literacy (e.g., eighth-grade students will design and conduct an independent scientific inquiry), and the strategic plan will detail how that goal is to be achieved.

The planning process for the district and schools starts with the premise that the board's priorities will be addressed. Once the vision planning process is complete, the board endorses this statement; this endorsement provides additional direction for the development of an excellence agenda to implement the vision.

Planning the Excellence Agenda

When the district's priorities and vision statement have been voted on by the board, excellence agenda planning begins. The agenda extends the vision statement (a statement of two to three paragraphs) by establishing specific goals to be achieved by students; it makes the general elements of a vision statement explicit in terms of specific student outcomes. In essence, the excellence agenda deals with *what* students should know and be able to do. The agenda also suggests specific programs or initiatives that might be used to achieve the goals (e.g., Drop Everything and Read Program). The strategic plan, the next step in the process, will express *how* the agenda is to be implemented over a span of time.

The superintendent oversees the process by convening a steering committee to develop the excellence agenda. Then, the superintendent and the steering committee solicit (and recruit as necessary) volunteers to organize working committees to produce the planning documents. The steering committee should be made up of professional staff from within the district and representatives of parents and the community. Each stakeholder group should be represented.

Steering committees of this type tend to organize subcommittees around specific topics identified by the priorities and the vision statement; the subcommittees produce the excellence agenda. The number of subcommittees is dictated by the topics to be covered, such as professional development, assessment of learning, governance, community involvement, and so forth. Depending on the vision statement, specific subject areas, such as science, might be addressed by a subcommittee. Each of the working subcommittees should be cochaired by a school district employee and a person not employed by the district. The district representative understands how the school system operates and can access information needed by the working committee; the "outside" person represents stakeholder groups who have a vested interest in the school district.

The steering committee, working with the superintendent, oversees the overall process of developing the excellence agenda. This steering committee approves the timetable for planning,

receives interim and final reports from each working committee,

makes recommendations to the superintendent, and

reviews drafts of the final report that will be sent to the board.

Each working subcommittee solicits volunteers from the school district and the stakeholder community. Each committee may also recruit specialists from the district or the community to provide expertise required to complete the planning task. The superintendent assumes the executive authority to ensure that each committee is representative of the district and the community with respect to issues such as gender, race, academic levels, and so forth.

To make sure that the planning process proceeds efficiently, the superintendent appoints a planning coordinator who provides the day-to-day assistance required by the working committees. To ensure that the planning process gets off to a good start, the coordinator prepares a planning guide for each working committee, which proposes a mission statement for that committee and suggests questions that can be used to get the planning process started.

The mission statement and the lead questions are not intended to be prescriptive; rather, they help initiate the planning process. Each subcommittee is free to change the mission statement or the lead questions and develop its own process to produce the planning documents. The only requirements are that (a) the planning process address the board's priorities and (b) the product is consistent with the vision statement approved by the board. Each subcommittee can establish its own meeting times and places, provided that they meet the deadlines established by the steering committee for interim and final reports.

The planning coordinator is responsible for several important functions, such as the following:

- Maintaining frequent contact with the cochairs of the subcommittees to ensure that the planning process is progressing according to schedule
- Keeping the superintendent informed of the progress and any problems that are being encountered
- Ensuring that each subcommittee communicates with appropriate resource personnel within the district to ensure that planning is reasonable and consistent with the district's practices

- Providing each subcommittee with guidelines for the preparation of the interim and final reports
- Ensuring that the committees are preparing their reports in a consistent manner so that major rewriting does not have to be done
- Blending the final reports from each committee into the comprehensive plan for the board to approve

The proposed excellence agenda, which emerges from the efforts of all the subcommittees, makes explicit the implicit goals of the vision statement. The agenda document specifies (a) the goals to be achieved by students and the school district, (b) suggested activities to be implemented to achieve those goals, and (c) the criteria that will be used to judge goal attainment. The excellence agenda is the first step in developing a strategic plan.

The strategic plan describes the specific time-referenced schedule for the excellence agenda's implementation (usually 3 to 5 years) and the budget required. The plan is developed by the planning coordinator and appropriate central office staff members, based on the agenda outlined. Significant milestones are identified in the plan to guide the board and those who will implement the plan. Milestones identify key events or outcomes that can be used to judge the progress being made. (Achieving the milestones provides opportunities for the entire district and the community to recognize and confirm partial or full attainment of goals.) When completed, the proposed excellence agenda and strategic plan are presented to the board for their formal adoption.

The superintendent must inform the board, the staff, and the community about the progress made in implementing the excellence agenda and strategic plan. Regular newsletters produced by the district can be used for this purpose; however, due to the special nature and the importance of the effort, an exclusive periodic publication should be considered. Information must flow to the board, the entire district, and the community to announce and describe the activities undertaken to improve education in the school district.

Maintaining interest in and promoting the agenda with the board can be accomplished in several ways: For example, the board should be (a) invited to make site visits to observe the excellence agenda in action and (b) provided with specific information that helps them trace the results of their policy deliberations and budget decisions. Such opportunities bring the abstract process of policy making to a point where board members can see the results of their actions in classrooms. Members of the steering committee should also be invited to make school visits so that they can view firsthand the results of their work. The professional staff members also need opportunities to observe what is going on in the schools to implement the agenda; it must be remembered that teachers are often isolated in their classrooms and need to be informed as much as any other stakeholder group.

The superintendent exerts the role of advocate for the excellence agenda by keeping it on the front burner for the board, staff, and community. By constantly referring to the agenda, the superintendent affirms its importance and provides a focus for the professionals, the board, and the community.

This chapter has described the role of the superintendent as a data-oriented educational leader. Chapter 8 provides two specific examples of needs assessment data and how they were used to facilitate decision-making processes and educational improvements.

SUMMARY

The needs assessment survey is an important way to initiate an excellence agenda; it also provides the basis for the superintendent to exercise data-oriented educational leadership. Through the careful analysis of existing information and the perceptions of needs by all stakeholder groups, the superintendent is in the best position to launch an agenda. The needs assessment survey provides the opportunity for the superintendent and the stakeholders to reflect on the conditions that can and should be improved to achieve excellence for the district.

Following the needs assessment survey, the board, with the guidance of the superintendent, establishes priorities. The priorities serve as the parameters for the development of a vision statement. The superintendent engages all stakeholder groups in the development of a vision statement that describes the district's aspirations for its students. The board adopts the vision statement as a measure of its commitment to achieve excellence. Following the adoption of the vision statement, the superintendent convenes a steering committee to help oversee the development of plans to implement the vision. With the steering committee, the superintendent organizes a number of subcommittees to build the actual plans to implement the vision. The plan that emerges from this process becomes the proposed excellence agenda; a strategic plan will put the agenda into operation. Most important, the excellence agenda specifies the criteria that will be used to judge progress toward the ultimate attainment of the goals of excellence. The board formally votes approval of the excellence agenda, the strategic plan, and the budget to support it as the way to implement the district's vision.

The participative process by which the needs assessment is planned and carried out builds commitment for what will become the excellence agenda. By engaging all stakeholder groups in developing the detailed plans, the superintendent ensures that the final agenda reflects the commitment of a broad group of constituents. By engaging the professionals and the community in establishing the excellence agenda, the superintendent confirms the important role of the superintendent as the educational leader.

CHAPTER

4

Improving and Assessing
Student Learning Outcomes

The basic skills of education—reading, writing, speaking, computing—
provide pupils with the tools to learn. Becoming educated depends on the
ability to use these tools to decode printed material, communicate both
orally and in writing, use number operations, and gain meaning from new
experiences.

The conditions required to improve learning outcomes are that students (a) experience an environment where they are respected, treated fairly
by adults, and actively engaged in the learning process; (b) become actively
involved in the life and the work of the school; (c) are guided to perceive
the relevance of schooling to life outside of school and graduate from high
school; and (d) are prepared with academic and personal skills and dispositions for the successful transition from school to work or postsecondary
education.

Improving Student Outcomes

Command of the basic skills enables students to apply those skills to problem solving as well as to analysis, synthesis, and evaluation of information. Higher-order thinking skills are an important goal for pupils to become self-initiating, self-directing, lifelong learners. All children and youths, especially minority and poor children, need opportunities to acquire these thinking skills to increase the probability of becoming educated people.

Achieving higher-order thinking skills requires that both teachers and pupils commit to this level of teaching and learning in a positive, supportive environment. The substance of education requires that pupils use basic and higher-order thinking skills to acquire meanings and to synthesize information and experiences; this forms the basis of the academic disciplines.

The Superintendent's Role
in Improving Student Outcomes

The superintendent's responsibilities with respect to student acquisition of basic and higher-order thinking skills center on the following:

- Ensuring that proper instruction programs are in place to promote achievement of basic and higher-order thinking skills
- Installing achievement monitoring systems to assure pupils, parents, guardians, teachers, and principals that learning has taken place
- Taking appropriate action to be sure that faculty and administration are dedicated to the development of higher-order thinking in the education of children and youths
- Ensuring that principals provide for appropriate instructional materials for teachers so that students attain basic skills and higher-order thinking goals.

The Importance of Basic Skills Acquisition

The emphasis in primary grade education is to provide students with the skills that are tools for further learning. The future success of children in school is dictated largely by their command of these skills at the end of the primary grades. Therefore, it is important that superintendents (a) pay close attention to the achievement of basic skills in primary grade pupils and (b) establish the expectation that pupils will be exposed to learning situations that involve problem solving and higher-order thinking.

Intermediate grades require pupils to use the tool skills to further their education. Reading to learn becomes the major focus at this stage. Beyond middle school, students need to extend their learning skills to more sophisticated levels. Teachers must offer a variety of learning experiences that actively engage students in problem-solving activities and promote higher-order thinking skills.

Monitoring Student Growth in Basic Skills Achievement

Because basic skills lay the foundation for student success in school and in life, the superintendent needs to monitor student achievement; he or she needs to assure parents and the community that students are achieving these skills as they progress throughout their schooling. Teachers need to be able to monitor student growth and communicate to parents in a timely manner that their children are mastering the tool skills. Teachers need ongoing information about student progress to make necessary modifications in instruction to ensure student mastery of these basis skills.

Data gathered at periodic intervals to monitor student progress need to be analyzed so that appropriate interventions can be designed for reteaching, additional practice, acceleration, or tutoring. This diagnostic approach exemplifies the essence of differentiated pedagogy described in Chapters 1 and 5. To assist all teachers and principals in adequately monitoring student progress, a school district may need an achievement monitoring system (see Chapter 9).

Basic skills mastery is so vital to a child's education and future life success that school districts must guarantee that virtually every child achieves mastery of them. At the school level, the principal as the educational leader must assure all children and their parents that he or she will monitor students' progress and ensure their mastery of these critical tool skills. At the district level, the superintendent as the educational leader must ensure that support systems to promote mastery of the basic skills are in place and operating effectively. The superintendent needs adequate monitoring information to be assured that this important task is given the attention it needs.

How to Develop an Achievement Monitoring System for Basic Skills

The development of an achievement monitoring system for basic skills requires the following steps:

1. Clear delineation of the expectations of what students are to learn at each level of schooling

2. Selection of a limited number of outcomes that are critical to student success at each level of education

3. Provision of examples of student work that satisfactorily meet the criteria so that students, teachers, and parents understand the expected learning outcomes

4. Validation of criterion outcomes by comparison with the work of relevant national associations (e.g., National Council of Mathematics Teachers)

5. Identification or development of test items that reflect those outcomes

6. Organization of test items into monitoring instruments that can be administered periodically

7. Cultivation of the understanding that testing is a natural component of the instructional process and need not be a traumatic event

8. Examination of instructional materials to determine their adequacy in achieving basic skills attainment

9. Acquisition of additional materials if needed

10. Provision of appropriate training for teachers so that they understand the monitoring system

11. Implementation of monitoring to ensure that teachers carry out their responsibilities for diagnostic instruction and data interpretation for instructional planning

12. Provision of appropriate training for principals to ensure that they understand their responsibilities for the achievement monitoring system and make appropriate interventions to promote student mastery

13. Offer of appropriate training for parents so that they understand the role that they can play in helping their children master the tool skills of learning

14. Dissemination of information to parents specifying how their children are progressing in the achievement of basic skills

The superintendent needs to oversee the development and implementation of an achievement monitoring system so that the school district can fulfill its responsibility to students. Chapter 9 gives a specific example of a monitoring system to improve student achievement.

Advantages and Disadvantages of Achievement Monitoring

There are three major advantages to achievement monitoring systems. First, they provide a virtual guarantee to parents and their children that the tool skills of learning will be addressed and mastered.

Second, a monitoring system provides a framework for teachers, administrators, and parents to talk about children's progress. The periodic reports that parents receive give them a continuous record of their child's progress in achieving the critical tool skills of learning.

Third, achievement monitoring allows teachers to (a) analyze progress and plan instruction accordingly; (b) make provisions for reteaching, additional practice, advancement, or regrouping of students for instruction and peer tutoring; and (c) provide developmentally appropriate instruction.

The major disadvantage of achievement monitoring of basic skills is that it may promote an overemphasis on the lower-level skills. If teachers focus exclusively on basic skills, they may overemphasize repetitive drill and deny students the opportunity to engage in higher-order thinking. If used inappropriately, frequent achievement monitoring may be viewed as excessive testing.

The Importance of Developing Higher-Order Thinking Skills

Developing higher-order thinking skills, which facilitate the ability to perceive relationships, is central to the pursuit of excellence in education. The ability to see how things are related to each other and the disposition for thoughtfulness is, according to Newmann (1991b), a hallmark of the educated person.

The development of these skills presupposes the ability to decode information and communicate effectively. In recent decades, many programs have been developed to promote the acquisition of higher-order thinking skills. Many of these deal with the exercise of general thinking skills not related to any specific academic subject. Bruer (1993), in his review of cognitive development in schoolchildren, points out that efforts to promote general higher-order thinking skills have usually proved ineffective. Recent research has focused on the ability of novices and experts to create meaning in specific academic contexts. Expert performance in a specific field, Bruer notes, requires knowledge of the subject matter, general learning and thinking skills, and the ability to monitor one's thinking; generalized thinking skills alone do not enable one to learn effectively in a specific academic discipline.

Higher-order thinking skills in specific academic disciplines are directed toward students making new knowledge—their ability to create new meanings for themselves as a result of educational experiences. This is usually represented by the creation of products, such as papers, diagrams, or models, that reflect the newly acquired insights.

Teaching for Higher-Order Thinking

One perspective for teaching higher-order thinking skills is framed by the concepts of authentic teaching, learning, and assessment developed by Newmann and his colleagues. Newmann and Wehlage (1993) identify five criteria for authentic instruction:

1. Higher-order thinking
2. Depth of knowledge
3. Connectedness to the world beyond the classroom
4. Substantive conversation
5. Social support for student achievement

Higher-order thinking can be contrasted with lower-order thinking: In lower-order thinking, students are expected to recite factual information that they have been told or have read—no interpretation of the information is expected; higher-order thinking requires students to analyze and integrate information to make meaning for themselves.

Depth of knowledge refers to the substance of the ideas taught. Knowledge is thin or superficial, according to Newmann (1992), when it (a) does not deal with the concepts or generalizations in a specific topic or discipline and (b) deals with trivial information. Knowledge is deep when it deals with the central concepts and complex understandings of an academic discipline. To engage in higher-order thinking, students need to deal in depth with a specific topic or discipline.

Connectedness to the world beyond the classroom refers to the meaning that instruction has beyond the school experience and setting. Lessons gain authenticity to the extent that instructional activities engage the student; students need to perceive relationships between topics studied and external social contexts (Newmann, 1992). When explicit references are made to external social and economic contexts, students are more likely to perceive the relevance of learning to subsequent work life.

Substantive conversation refers to student engagement in extended discussion with their peers in response to questions posed by the teacher; the teacher guides the discourse. Students use complete sentences and build on one another's understanding of topics under discussion. Substantive conversation is contrasted with lecture and recitation-type instruction where the teacher talks and students listen and respond to questions with one word or a few words (Newmann, 1992). To engage in substantive conversation, students must explore depth of knowledge and engage in higher-order thinking.

Social support for student achievement refers to the teacher's creating a classroom environment with high expectations for all students, encouraging student participation in discussions and praising student engagement in difficult learning tasks (Newmann, 1992).

When teachers support students taking risks in classes and urge them to try hard to master challenging work, they create the climate of respect and encouragement that students need. Many students have been socialized in educational environments where they have not engaged in substantive conversation or higher-order thinking. They will need the nurturing support of teachers to try more challenging approaches to learning.

Authentic Assessment of Student Learning

The development of higher-order thinking as proposed by Newmann and reviewed by Bruer emphasizes both different types of instruction and different ways of assessing learning. Much has been written about *authentic assessment* by Archbald and Newmann (1988) and others. It is best described by contrasting it with conventional standardized tests. Standardized tests and text-embedded tests overwhelmingly test lower-level skills (Madaus, 1992), which typically require only recall of information or the unthinking application of algorithms in mathematics. Higher-order skills, on the other hand, require students to apply lower-level skills to situations not previously encountered. Authentic assessment strives to present students with testing situations that require them to apply knowledge and skills to solve problems or create new meanings.

Authentic assessment tasks may require students to manipulate materials in science, for example, and generate findings based on experimentation. In social studies, authentic assessment is illustrated by the document-based questions in the College Board's advanced placement exams for secondary schools. These questions typically provide students with information from two sources that may be in conflict with one another or two different perspectives on a particular event. Students are asked to compare and contrast information, draw conclusions, and use additional knowledge they have acquired to write an essay prompted by the question. The types of tasks presented to secondary students in document-based questions can be modified for children at the elementary and middle school levels to promote higher-order thinking. In authentic assessment exercises, students create new knowledge for themselves by responding to questions that they have not previously encountered.

Archbald and Newmann (1988) define authentic assessment of student learning as dealing with (a) production of knowledge, (b) disciplined inquiry, and (c) value beyond evaluation.

Production of knowledge refers to the student making new meaning for himself or herself, perceiving relationships between the information that has been encountered and constructing new meanings. It refers to the development of new insights by a student, not to the student actually creating new knowledge for a specific discipline.

Disciplined inquiry refers to using prior knowledge, developing an in-depth understanding of that knowledge, and integrating it in a way that creates new meaning for the student.

Value beyond evaluation refers to that quality of assessment that goes beyond the mere validation of student acquisition of knowledge. It means that a student's authentic product manifests his or her understanding of a topic or discipline; it also means that the product has some utilitarian, aesthetic, or personal value for the student beyond the demonstration of competence. Therefore, the product of student learning can be applied and has some value in the world beyond the classroom.

Instructional Materials for Authentic Teaching

Most textbooks in American classrooms are not appropriate for authentic instruction and assessment, typically providing students with conclusions reached by authors rather than allowing students to make their own meaning after gaining background knowledge. Although necessary for presentation of background information, they are usually not suitable for authentic instruction. To produce new knowledge or make meaning for themselves, students should use primary source material requiring them to draw their own conclusions.

Teacher Training for
Authentic Instruction and Assessment

This section might be more appropriate in the chapter on professional development (see Chapter 5), but it is included here because of its specific relationship to higher-order thinking and authentic assessment.

Authentic instruction and assessment require specific teaching skills that many teachers in American schools may not yet have been trained to use. Science teachers who use inductive teaching methods may have the skills to engage students in meaning making based on effective laboratory methods of instruction. More often than not, however, teachers tend to use more didactic methods of instruction because such methods tend to fit the time allotted in the school schedule. Curriculum guidelines and textbooks can provide barriers to authentic instruction. Teachers are expected to follow districtwide curriculum guides, which tend to emphasize broad coverage of material rather than studying a few topics in depth. Textbooks tend to provide extensive material covering various topics; this exerts additional pressure for teachers to cover the ground. Thus, the two important tools given to teachers—guides and textbooks—typically do not enable them to use authentic instruction or assessment.

Organizations such as Sizer's Coalition of Essential Schools at Brown University encourage and support teachers in their quest for "less is more" (Sizer, 1984); this motto of the coalition encourages teachers to engage their students in studying a few topics in great depth rather than attempting to cover broad surveys of knowledge. For teachers to create materials supporting authentic instruction requires considerable effort.

Guiding the learning process with authentic instruction means that teachers will involve students in extensive classroom dialogue and support student inquiry. It requires teachers to frame questions that may not have any predetermined right answers. Engaging students in sustained dialogue and tolerating the ambiguity that such authentic teaching requires are not easy tasks. More important, many teachers have not experienced authentic instruction in their own preparation programs nor have they been hired for or oriented to a position that typically requires this type of teaching. Thus, a significant staff development program would have to be organized to train and coach teachers to teach authentically, develop and use authentic assessment measures, and create learning tasks that would require authentic student work.

The long-range ideal would be having new teachers skilled in authentic teaching methods. This would require training institutions to use these methods in their teacher preparation programs, including practice in using these methods in student teaching experiences. Teachers need to be skilled in creating problem-centered learning tasks for students and in guiding learning rather than using lectures as the predominant mode of instruction. Such expectations for teacher educators indicate significant faculty development programs at colleges and universities—a major undertaking for institutions engaged in teacher preparation.

The Superintendent's Role in Promoting Authentic Teaching, Learning, and Assessment

It is the superintendent who has to create the conditions that support and promote higher-order thinking skills and authenticity in instruction, assessment, and learning. Creating such conditions may necessitate a significant cultural shift both within schools and in the community. Teachers and the general public tend to verbalize the need for developing higher-order thinking skills in pupils; creating the conditions to bring them about may call for significant changes.

Outcome-Based Education and the Right Wing

Some organizations, active in some communities, reflect the values of the conservative right wing and do not want pupils to acquire critical thinking skills that might encourage them to challenge established authority or family and community values. Others express concern that approaches such as outcome-based education tend to promote liberal values that undermine the family and religious beliefs. Such conservative right-wing groups want their own traditional knowledge, values, and skills taught to their children (Clarkson & Porteous, 1993).

It is generally acknowledged that in some states, conservative groups attempt to implement their values in the following ways:

- Target school board elections to ensure that their values are protected, outcome-based education is opposed, and schools will not stray from traditional instructional methods and values

- Seek to elect school board members who will influence policy decisions, textbook adoptions, and personnel decisions
- Mount platforms to rid school districts of certain teachers and administrators, especially superintendents
- Use questionable election tactics, such as antitax platforms to gain popular support when, in reality, they have a much more pointed objective in influencing the content of instruction and specific values
- Take the position that they are against the teaching of values in the schools when, in reality, they are more interested in teaching values to which they subscribe
- Focus their opposition on values issues

Most parents and community members accept the goals of outcome-based education related to academic content and skills, once they have been explained to them. Most citizens want students to read, write, speak, and solve problems. Given the context described earlier, superintendents need to exercise care in framing initiatives relating to higher-order thinking and outcome-based education to focus on the real issues of promoting and verifying student competence in academic and learning skills.

Superintendents will have to develop strategies that encourage communities to think about their children's need to compete in the economy of the 21st century. These strategies must focus on the type of work that parents and educators want students to produce as a result of their education. When parents can see examples of student work that represent authentic learning, they are more likely to agree with that concept. Broad consensus among educators and parents is needed to promote the goals of authentic teaching and learning.

The Superintendent's Role

The superintendent's role in promoting the goal of authentic teaching, learning, and assessment is to

1. articulate to all stakeholder groups the need for students to be taught to be effective problem solvers;
2. create awareness of the need for professional development training for teachers and administrators;

3. engage in discussions with education professionals, parents, and community leaders to promote understanding and acceptance of such goals; and

4. remain informed about developments on the national scene that may help the school district reach its goal of authenticity in student work.

Student Assessment

The National Council of Teachers of Mathematics was the first professional group to set new standards for student achievement (in math). Other national associations (e.g., National Council for Social Studies) are identifying similar outcomes. The New Standards Project sponsored by the National Alliance for School Restructuring is an intensive effort to establish a new system of student assessment for the nation. The New Standards Project (see Chapter 8) is working to set world-class standards in each subject area for American students (Simmons & Resnick, 1993). Once the standards are delineated, the project proposes to develop national examinations as models for state and local school districts to adopt or adapt to their needs and instructional sequences to achieve the standards proposed. Currently, the project is working on protocols for the evaluation of student writing and mathematics. Superintendents are well-advised to follow closely the ongoing work of this group.

Eliminating Barriers to Higher-Order Thinking

A superintendent can take three positive steps to eliminate barriers to and promote achievement of higher-order thinking skills. First, develop communitywide support for the development of critical thinking skills in students. Second, provide teachers with training to ensure that they have a command of the teaching repertoires to implement these skills. Third, develop the ability of principals and subject supervisors to assist teachers in implementing classroom instruction designed to promote these thinking skills.

Support for Problem-Solving Thinking

Most business people I have talked to want to employ high school graduates who can read, write, speak, listen, follow directions, solve problems, and get along with fellow workers. In addition, they want workers who have a positive work ethic and will come to work regularly and on time. These are universally desired skills and dispositions; the school has a responsibility to promote them.

Of greatest interest to business people is the ability of their employees to solve problems. Problem solving is similar to the critical or higher-order thinking presented earlier. It is the ability to analyze problems, generate alternative solutions, test hypotheses, and implement and evaluate solutions. Higher-order thinking skills of analysis, synthesis, and evaluation are central to problem solving.

Most adults will not be opposed to teaching problem solving or higher-order thinking skills when they are explained in this real-world context. The subject matter chosen to develop these skills, however, can cause problems. Using controversial social or political issues as the subject matter for development of critical thinking skills is fraught with problems. Even though educators may have positive motivations for using such topics—because the issues are controversial and are subject to rich analysis—teachers' motives can often be misunderstood. It is relatively easy to develop skills such as detecting bias and noting contradictions in positions by examining current social or political issues; but no matter how such matters are handled in the classroom, some parents and community members may see educators using such issues to promote a particular point of view. To the extent that such issues border on moral dilemmas, they are guaranteed to promote controversy that may have a detrimental effect on the goal of developing higher-order thinking. Dealing with historical dilemmas may also have its problems depending on the specific subject and how it is approached.

There are many opportunities, such as science and mathematics problems as well as analysis of carefully selected literature, where these important problem-solving skills can be developed. Developing young people's thinking skills is too important a task to open the process up to potential criticism by carelessly selecting the subject matter used to promote those skills.

Developing Teaching Skills for Higher-Order Thinking

If teaching for higher-order thinking skills is viewed as a necessary ingredient for the educated person, why is it not more evident in our schools? Several possible reasons are that (a) these skills are difficult to teach, (b) many teachers have not been trained to develop and promote higher-order thinking skills, (c) instructional materials often do not lend themselves to this purpose, (d) conventional testing instruments (on which a school's reputation may be judged) don't test for these skills, and (e) a systematic staff development program has not been implemented.

To promote higher-order thinking skills, the superintendent will have to ensure that the following actions are taken:

- Instructional materials will have to be purchased that lend themselves to the development of these skills
- Instructional materials will have to be developed by teachers in curriculum development workshops
- Test items and examinations will have to be developed to assess the outcomes of higher-order thinking

Unfortunately, the schedules of many American schools tend to work against the development of higher-order thinking skills. Problem-solving learning takes more time than didactic instruction: It takes more time for teachers to create problem-solving learning environments, and it takes more time for students to engage in problem-solving learning. Also, many teachers are unaccustomed to and uncomfortable in using this type of pedagogy. Unfortunately, teachers have been socialized in a profession where they are expected to know the right answers to student questions. Problem-solving situations, however, may have many right answers or no right answers and require teachers to tolerate ambiguity, ask probing questions, and guide students through a learning experience rather than tell them the answer. These teaching behaviors often take more time than that allotted in the typical school schedule.

Newmann (1991b) asserts that creating a disposition for classroom thoughtfulness is one of the great needs in promoting authentic teaching and authentic student work. Teachers need to model thoughtfulness for students; they will need to organize learning experiences to provide time for students to reflect on what they have learned and to explore relationships to prior knowledge. Teachers need encouragement from their colleagues to create the conditions for classroom thoughtfulness. The superintendent will have to put forth expectations for teachers to promote classroom thoughtfulness and provide appropriate training. The district will have to adopt policies and practices that deemphasize the broad coverage of instructional topics and encourage teachers and students to study a few areas in great depth.

SUMMARY

The superintendent's role in improving student outcomes begins with ensuring that the students in the district master the basic skills of learning so that they can become lifelong learners. A monitoring system for basic skills attainment can help achieve this goal by focusing the attention of teachers, parents, and students on mastery of these skills. The major potential disadvantage is that it may tend to overemphasize attention on basic skills attainment.

The superintendent also leads the professional staff to ensure that all students, especially minority children, are given opportunities to develop higher-order thinking skills. Authentic methods of teaching, learning, and assessment promote higher-order thinking, depth of knowledge, substantive conversation for students, connectedness to the world beyond the classroom, and social support for student learning. Authentic assessment requires students to demonstrate that they have made meaning from learning experiences by producing new knowledge for themselves.

The superintendent's role in promoting and assessing higher-order learning outcomes for students requires building support among stakeholders. It further requires communicating the need for professional training and the need to develop instructional and assessment techniques. Finally, the superintendent will have to work with the board to adopt policies and financial resources that support the implementation of educational experiences for students to achieve higher-order learning outcomes.

CHAPTER

5

Comprehensive Evaluation
and Professional Development
of Principals and Teachers

Two issues fundamental to the superintendent's role as an educational leader are evaluation of personnel and professional development. My view is that the primary purpose of evaluation is to provide feedback to improve the leadership and pedagogical skills of professionals; a secondary purpose is to make summary judgments about the overall quality of professional performance. Professional development is fundamental for two reasons. First, it sets the expectation that professionals will work continuously to improve their performance as leaders and teachers. Second, comprehensive systematic staff development programs can offer principals and teachers the knowledge and skills required to move forward the district's excellence agenda. Both goals have a direct influence on improved student achievement.

The superintendent has four major responsibilities regarding evaluation and professional development:

1. To develop and implement a comprehensive evaluation system for principals and teachers
2. To define the role of the principal as an educational leader and identify the elements of a professional development program to achieve this goal
3. To develop and implement a continuing professional development program for teachers to enhance their pedagogical skills
4. To create the climate to support effective personnel evaluation and professional development

Together, performance evaluation and professional development form the basis for maintaining a dynamic community of learners among the district's professionals. For the purposes of this book, the terms *professional development* and *staff development* are used interchangeably. When educational professionals continue to improve their leadership and pedagogical skills, they reach the cutting edge of their profession in pursuit of achieving an excellence agenda.

Developing and Implementing
a Comprehensive Evaluation System

Based on my experience, the process of establishing an effective comprehensive personnel evaluation system involves

establishing criteria for professional performance,

orienting and training all professionals so that they understand the expectations for their roles,

supplying specific skill training where needed,

providing feedback (formative evaluation) to improve the quality of performance, and

reaching summative judgments and communicating results.

The major concepts of each component in this process are summarized in the following sections.

Establishing Criteria

The first step in developing a comprehensive evaluation system is specifying the general and specific performance criteria for each professional role. General criteria set forth the areas for expected performance (e.g., educational leadership for principals); specific criteria provide more detailed expectations (e.g., observes and confers with teachers to improve instruction).

Lists of expected behaviors for principals and teachers can be found in the educational literature; however, a local district's criteria need to be developed with input from those who will be measured by them. The criteria are useful because they (a) establish the goals for expected performance, (b) contain implicitly or explicitly the means that will be used to judge the quality of performance, (c) set the stage for formative and summative evaluation, and (d) imply the type of training needed to promote the desired performance.

Providing Orientation and Training

Once the performance criteria are established, the professionals need orientation and training to understand the expectations set for them. It cannot be assumed that each member of a professional group will assign the same meaning to a statement of expectations, particularly if new ones are being established. For example, teachers may be expected to use techniques consistent with differentiated pedagogy; in that case, they will undoubtedly require some orientation and training to understand the language that expresses the expectations. Similarly, if principals are expected to function as educational leaders, they will need orientation and training to ensure that the intended meanings of the role expectations are fully understood.

Supplying Skill Training

Once the role expectations are understood, professionals should receive appropriate training in the skills and knowledge they need to fulfill them. Assume, for example, that teachers are given the new expectation of using higher-order questioning and active learning in their classrooms; they may need demonstrations, skill training, observation, feedback, and follow-up coaching to acquire the skills on which they will be evaluated.

Giving Feedback

After a principal has been trained in observing and conferring skills, a supervisor needs to observe that principal engaged in a teacher observation and as he or she plans and conducts a conference with that teacher. The supervisor completes the process by giving feedback to the principal that is designed to improve his or her performance. Direct observation and feedback are cornerstones of any personnel evaluation system intended to improve professional performance.

Reaching Summative Judgments and Communicating Results

Summative evaluation is used to judge the ability of a professional to perform the tasks stated in the performance criteria. For example, principals should be evaluated on their ability to lead faculty in the analysis of educational trends—one of the criteria for educational leadership. An evaluative judgment has to be made by the supervisor based on actual observation of the principal engaging the faculty in the analysis of trends. Assume that a staff development trainer communicates to a supervisor that a principal is doing an effective or ineffective job in involving faculty members in trend analysis; the supervisor cannot make a summative judgment based on that secondhand evidence. He or she must actually observe the principal engaged in trend analysis with the teachers.

Such practices are fair and necessary from the legal viewpoint of due process; when reaching a negative judgment about the effectiveness of a teacher or principal, the superintendent must demonstrate that due process has been afforded the individual. If, for example, a principal is unable to reach the expected level of educational leadership, the district may have to demote or dismiss him or her. The district needs to document that it provided the principal with a reasonable amount of training and extensive formative evaluation; if the principal is still unable to be an effective educational leader, the district will have established the conditions for demotion or dismissal.

A comprehensive evaluation system should include all five of the foregoing components. Implementing a district evaluation system without paying careful attention to each of these steps may be both unprofessional and illegal. Educational professionals have a right to (a) know what is expected of them, (b) receive training to orient them to the evaluative criteria established for their positions, (c) expect training to acquire any skills necessary to meet new performance requirements, (d) expect formative evaluations to improve the quality of their performance based on direct observation of their performance coupled with the evaluative criteria established for their positions, and (e) expect that summative judgments made about the quality of their performance will result from direct observation.

If superintendents take seriously the evaluation of professional performance to achieve an excellence agenda, an effective comprehensive evaluation system will assist that undertaking. The presence of such a system lends credibility to a school district; the absence of one casts doubts on a district's effectiveness.

Developing the Role of
Principal as Educational Leader

Just as the superintendent is the educational leader for the district, the principal is the educational leader for the school. The principal, responsible for student achievement, must make the education of pupils the top priority in meeting the goals of an excellence agenda. Teachers, individually and collectively, are technically responsible for the achievement of each student; however, the principal has the obligation to assure parents and the community that students are achieving the established learning goals. The principal must demonstrate (a) that proper conditions exist to support teaching and learning and (b) that teachers are fulfilling their obligations for instruction and assessment of student learning.

The role of the principal as educational leader has been articulated by the profession only since the 1970s. Also, only during this period did parents and the general public begin to expect principals to play this role. Prior to that time, most principals were trained in and expected to provide managerial functions to support school operations. To meet current expectations, veteran principals may need to acquire new knowledge and skills to function effectively.

Superintendents must ensure that professional development programs are in place to prepare veteran principals to function as educational leaders. Such programs can be developed jointly by higher education institutions and local school districts.

Criteria for educational leadership (a) are the foundation for the comprehensive evaluation of principals and (b) foreshadow the content of a professional development program. These criteria, designed to ultimately improve student learning outcomes, require that the principal

1. lead faculty and parents in achieving consensus on shared values and building a shared vision for the school;

2. observe and confer with teachers to improve instruction;

3. monitor student achievement;

4. create a positive climate for students, teachers, parents, and community;

5. maintain knowledge of recent research and trends in instruction and learning;

6. understand recent developments in student assessment;

7. lead the faculty in keeping abreast of recent trends in curriculum and instruction;

8. engage teachers in shared decision making in instructional matters; and

9. implement policies and provide support for teacher mentoring and coaching.

Descriptions of these expectations are provided in the following section.

Achieving Consensus on Shared Values and Building a Shared Vision

The vision-building process at the school level requires the principal to engage faculty and staff members as well as parents in extended dialogue to achieve consensus on their shared values. This parallels the process that the superintendent uses for the school district (see Chapter 3). These shared values form the basis for the school's vision statement and become the operating principles for the strategic plan to achieve the goal of excellence. In exploring common values held by the school's stakeholders, the principal may present this question: "What is the importance of the following topics in your vision of education?"

Knowledge, skills, attitudes, habits, and values

Academic, personal, and interpersonal skills

Group and independent work

Problem solving, risk taking, and adaptive skills

Learning how to learn and lifelong learning skills

Active and self-initiated learning

Self-evaluation and self-esteem

Developmentally appropriate instruction

Instruction relevant to students' needs and interests

A secure and caring environment

The principal and the stakeholders should add more issues to this illustrative, not definitive, list.

After discussions with stakeholders on such issues, principals should develop statements of beliefs that are shared in common; this, then, will form the basis for the school's vision of education for the common good. The principal leads the faculty, staff, and parents to develop a unique school vision that is consistent with the district's vision. The principal advocates for the school's and the district's vision, being a visible presence in the school and in direct contact with students, teachers, staff, and parents (Smith & Andrews, 1989); this can be accomplished in the classrooms, corridors, cafeteria, auditorium, and on the school grounds.

Observing and Conferring to Improve Instruction

Principals must allot sufficient time in their daily schedules to observe teachers in the classroom and confer with them to improve instruction. Unfortunately, many principals are not sufficiently prepared for this important task. To observe and confer effectively requires knowledge and training in clinical supervision or a comparable method. While observing a teaching episode, the principal takes notes to capture verbatim statements made by teachers and students. After analyzing the notes, the principal plans and conducts a conference to provide the teacher with (a) explicit feedback to reinforce effective teaching techniques and (b) suggestions to improve his or her performance. Verbatim notes are used to describe accurately instructional transactions that should be reinforced as well as techniques that need to be modified or discontinued.

Observing and conferring with teachers provides firsthand knowledge regarding the quality of interpersonal relations between the teacher and students. In addition, classroom observations and informal meetings with pupils allow the principal to know individual students and encourage them to do their best work. Firsthand observations of teacher classroom performance are mandatory for the principal who must make informed judgments about the quality of instruction.

Monitoring Student Achievement

The principal's careful monitoring of student achievement is the foundation for educational leadership; this is accomplished by carefully analyzing documentation, such as standardized achievement test results, criterion tests, department examinations, grades, and failure notices. For example, the principal should conduct item analyses of standardized achievement tests to determine the relative strengths and weaknesses of students in various subjects. Careful analysis may require a breakout of data by grade level, teacher, team, or other relevant variables.

Inadequate student performance can prompt a diagnostic analysis to identify underlying causes; in turn, this diagnosis can lead to generating alternatives to address the desired improvement. Careful consideration of test results can signal teachers and students that the principal is vitally interested in their progress as instructors and learners.

Grade distributions can provide principals with a great deal of information about their teachers. A skewing toward high or low grades can alert a principal that a problem may exist with a teacher. Further analysis may indicate that that teacher's expectations are inappropriately high or low for students or that the pacing of instruction is too fast or too slow.

Discussions with teachers, individually or in groups, about strengths and weaknesses in student performance, set the stage for educational improvement planning. Achievement monitoring contributes to the overall climate of high expectations for learning. Analyses of these data allow the principal to demonstrate a strong commitment to learning and the willingness to work with teachers to improve the quality of instruction. Most of all, it sets the high expectation that teachers will teach and students will learn.

Creating a Positive Climate for
Students, Teachers, Parents, and Community

Creating a positive climate for students. The principal plays a significant role in setting the school climate for students. Making clear the behavioral expectations for students and dealing with them in a consistently fair manner is essential. Through frequent informal meetings with students, the principal can demonstrate interest in their academic progress. For example, an elementary school principal may take time to have students come to the office and read. By doing this, the principal shows personal interest in each student's work and makes informal assessments of the growth of each pupil in reading achievement. Also, the principal can get to know the pupils and develop a positive rapport with them.

Through daily conversations with students in the school building and on the grounds, the principal can create a friendly yet firm relationship that sets expectations for a caring environment. Also, as he or she deals with individual pupils and their discipline problems, a climate of positive support is created for them to meet their own expectations as well as those of the school.

Creating a positive climate for teachers. To reach pedagogical maturity, described later in this chapter, teachers need an environment that stimulates and supports professional growth (Academy for Educational Development, 1985). The principal is responsible for creating such an environment and holds this expectation as the norm for all teachers. Nurturing teacher growth can be achieved in several ways, including, but not limited to, the following:

Stimulate discussions with teachers individually and in groups that cause them to examine their current practices and explore new techniques.

Structure faculty meetings to focus on instructional and curricular matters, not on "administrivia."

Meet with teachers in a department or a team to reflect on current practices and help them explore ways in which they might improve the quality of instruction and student achievement.

Meet with teachers individually to discuss their current professional activities and inquire how the principal might help them pursue additional instructional or curricular interests.

Stimulate interest in topics by bringing in articles from professional journals and asking teachers to react.

In general, the principal creates the climate for professional growth by developing and promoting a stimulating work environment. Frequent reference to educational matters lays the foundation for a climate fostering teachers' professional growth, which will in turn enhance student achievement.

Creating a positive climate for parents and community. Parents need to be greeted positively and treated with respect by all school personnel. They need to be appreciated for their efforts to help schools provide more effective services to pupils. The principal sets the tone by communicating expectations to staff and teachers about how parents and community members are to be integrated into the school. Engaging parents and community to support educational programs is one of the hallmarks of an educational leader. The principal needs to involve these stakeholders in collaborative planning to identify sources of support for educational programs.

As with other processes in which parents and community are involved, the principal needs to be skilled in running effective meetings and building consensus.

Parents, for the most part, are motivated to support the school in its educational endeavors. Community members are often willing to share their resources and talents so that schools can be more effective. Parent and community involvement in schools may not be without its problems, however. As in any human endeavor, personality conflicts and power struggles can arise that make working together difficult. Parents with a single-issue agenda or community members who advocate for a particular community action can cause problems for less experienced principals.

Principals may need training in conflict resolution to resolve effectively the differences that may arise among parents or community members. Principals need to understand the tactics that community activists use to achieve their agenda and, when necessary, intervene constructively to preserve the integrity of the school's mission and the attainment of its vision. By reaching out to the community and responding to reasonable requests from community groups, the principal creates goodwill and taps valuable community resources to help the school implement its vision.

Maintaining Knowledge of Educational Research and Trends

To exercise educational leadership, principals need to maintain current knowledge of curricula and instructional trends; this enables them to lead teachers to discover better or more efficient ways to promote student learning. Some ways this can be accomplished include

reading professional journals, doing research, attending conferences, and talking with specialists and supervisors in all instructional areas;

using the excellent teachers in their schools as resources; and

networking with principals in the district and the region to enhance current knowledge and seek advice in solving problems.

Understanding Recent and Emerging Developments in Student Assessment

The assessment of student learning affords a great opportunity for principals to show educational leadership. Educators and scholars are currently developing alternatives to standardized tests as the primary means of assessing student progress and achievement. The concepts of authentic testing and achievement, for example, characterize current efforts to align testing and assessment more closely with the types of student outcomes that educators value (Newmann, 1991a).

The New Standards Project discussed in Chapter 4 is another case in point. It establishes world-class standards for American students in critical academic areas and prepares examinations to assess student attainment of these standards. The assessment devices are intended to be models that state and local districts can adopt or adapt to verify student attainment of important learning goals.

Even though these two efforts in new assessments of student learning are still in the formative stages, a considerable body of literature exists on them. Principals can take advantage of current interest in assessment to engage faculty and parents in important discussions. The assessment of student achievement will continue to be of great importance to educators, parents, and the general public into the 21st century. Principals who keep informed on such issues will reach the cutting edge of much-needed reform in American education. In addition, as principals read, reflect, and talk with colleagues and the general public about student assessment, they enhance their roles as educational leaders.

Leading Faculty to Examine Trends

Principals must maintain current knowledge of curricular and instructional trends to guide faculty to consider innovations that might help implement their school's vision. Teachers also stay on the cutting edge of educational excellence by being knowledgeable about important trends.

Resource people, such as supervisors and subject matter specialists, should be invited to discuss new trends with teachers; then the principal can ask the faculty to reflect on whether any of them may be helpful in achieving their goals. For example, the principal may prompt the faculty to explore portfolio assessment as a means of effectively evaluating student progress; resource professionals within the district could make presentations on portfolio evaluation and assessment. Literature on portfolio assessment can also inform teachers about recent developments.

Teachers may have knowledge of research and trends to share with their peers and the principal. Those taking graduate courses can be a great source of information and expertise to help the principal and their peers stay abreast of new educational developments. As an educational leader, the principal's role is to orchestrate these activities and expose the faculty to trends that should be given serious consideration.

Building Shared Decision Making on Instructional Matters

The concept of shared decision making is important in developing a commitment to shared values. In practice, shared decision making among faculty fosters a willingness to accept responsibility for effective school operations. Principals should focus shared decision making on those matters that deal primarily with the educational program, such as the school schedule, selection of textbooks, reporting student progress to parents, and the like. Administrative matters that do not directly deal with instruction should be handled by the principal.

Requiring experienced principals to participate in shared decision making with their faculties may pose a challenge. Specific training can be given in this skill and may need to be followed by frequent observation and feedback to support the move from autocratic leadership to consensus decision making. The superintendent should monitor and support school-based shared decision making.

Implementing Mentoring and Coaching

Some states and many school districts have implemented formal mentoring programs for beginning teachers. The first few weeks of a teacher's career are vitally important in establishing the conditions for success. The principal can support a beginning teacher by carefully selecting and assigning a mentor teacher. A beginning teacher needs to know that the support of a mentor and the principal is available for getting off to a good start.

Mentoring and coaching teachers to reach their highest levels of performance should be a continual process. The principal sets the conditions and the expectations at the school level for this. He or she ensures that mentors and coaches are prepared and trained to perform their tasks and, through careful monitoring and support, ensures that such work with beginning teachers is successfully implemented. The superintendent's task is to provide principals with guidance, policies, and support for effective implementation of teacher mentoring and coaching.

Professional Development of Teachers

In the sections that follow, I discuss expectations for teachers' professional development and highlight the respective roles of principals and the superintendent in promoting these goals.

The quality of education in a school district is ultimately measured classroom by classroom, teacher by teacher. The variety of instructional strategies used and the quality of the interpersonal relationships between teachers and pupils in each classroom will determine the degree of excellence in a school district. Therefore, a superintendent must focus on improving the quality of pedagogy in all classrooms at all educational levels. Obviously, the day-to-day responsibility of carrying out the expectation for high-quality teaching belongs to principals at the school level and to central office personnel at the district level. The superintendent, however, must provide overall leadership and establish expectations to ensure that everything possible is done to help pupils receive the highest quality of instruction.

Focus on Differentiated Pedagogy

In Chapter 1, differentiated pedagogy was briefly introduced as an effective instructional technique; this section presents a detailed illustration of this concept. Differentiated pedagogy is one of the most sophisticated forms of instruction; it requires teachers to (a) carefully diagnose the stage of learning readiness for each of their pupils; (b) systematically plan instruction for individual students, groups of students, or the entire class based on the developmental readiness of the pupils and their current state of knowledge; and (c) constantly monitor student progress and change groupings of pupils and the content of instruction based on the developing state of knowledge and skill of each pupil (Academy for Educational Development, 1985).

In the following section, differentiated pedagogy is used to illustrate how the superintendent and the principal employ their leadership roles to improve instruction.

A Professional Development
Sequence for Differentiated Pedagogy

Differentiated pedagogy reflects an ideal state of professional development that all teachers should strive to reach. The superintendent can ensure that a comprehensive program of staff development is planned for all administrative and teaching staff. Teachers competent in the skills of differentiated pedagogy should participate in developing and carrying out the appropriate training for their peers. Live presentations, classroom observations, or well-prepared videotapes should be presented. For teachers, acquiring the skills of differentiated pedagogy should proceed as follows:

1. Become familiar with the language that describes the various aspects of differentiated pedagogy.
2. Understand the theoretical and practical rationales underlying this approach.
3. Observe models of differentiated pedagogy in action and analyze their implementation.
4. Receive training in its various components.
5. Practice the skills and receive feedback from observers.
6. Receive coaching and observation from peers, supervisors, and principals to ensure that the skills of differentiated pedagogy are integrated into their basic repertoire and used daily.

This brief description is a model of staff development described by Joyce and Showers (1988) and others in the field of professional development. The superintendent's role is to oversee such a program.

Concepts and Procedures for a Teacher Development Program in Differentiated Pedagogy

Some key concepts and procedures for such a program are (a) development of a common language, (b) diagnosis of learner readiness, (c) models of instruction, (d) peer observation and coaching, (e) focus on teachers in need, and (f) shared decision making for differentiated pedagogy. Examples of each follow.

Developing a common language. This requires understanding key terms and concepts of differentiated pedagogy. For example, teachers must fully understand the concept of developmentally appropriate instruction, which assumes that students have acquired the background knowledge and skills in which to integrate new learning experiences. Developing a common language takes several episodes of observation or training and the continual use and reinforcement of terms by peers, supervisors, and the principal.

Diagnosing learner readiness. This would seem to be a commonsense approach to teaching that all educators would use; this is not always the case. To diagnose the level of pupil readiness, a teacher needs to have a clear idea of the learning outcomes that a pupil should gain as a result of completing a particular course or subject. The teacher should also have access to formal data about each student's current state of knowledge or skills, available from scores on standardized tests or criterion tests in specific subjects. Informal data about students' current status may come from observations of their ability or inability to perform certain tasks. Teachers should be able to analyze formal and informal data to diagnose learner readiness and develop instructional plans for individuals or groups of students.

Usually, there are many fine teachers in school districts who accurately identify learner readiness. Skilled special education teachers, for example, tend to use highly effective diagnostic techniques to measure the readiness levels of their pupils in preparation for differentiating instruction. Competent athletic coaches also use sophisticated methods to pinpoint the current skill level of their players as a basis for planning practice sessions. Districts could use these two sources for teachers to observe effective diagnosis of learner readiness and ongoing monitoring of pupil development. The diagnosis of student readiness must be continuous. Once a teacher has determined the level of learning readiness and provided instruction, further assessment must occur for planning subsequent lessons.

Using models of instruction. Differentiated pedagogy assumes that the teacher has mastered a variety of instructional techniques and can select those most appropriate for particular students. A teacher development program may involve presentations or observations of different methods, such as (a) inquiry-oriented instruction in which students experiment and are led to discover underlying concepts or generalizations, (b) didactic instruction to provide students with a common background of information, and (c) cooperative team learning.

Teachers should possess a variety of instructional techniques to engage the interest in learning. Students become bored with the same strategies used over and over again.

Coaching and peer observation for mastery of techniques. Staff development research indicates that teachers need feedback and coaching to integrate new strategies into their ongoing expertise. They need opportunities to practice new methods in a safe environment and receive constructive feedback to master them. It may take more than 30 iterations for a new technique to become fully integrated into a teacher's instructional repertoire (Joyce & Showers, 1988).

Coaching can come from several sources. Staff development specialists can provide helpful feedback; principals who have been trained can also coach teachers to higher levels of performance. In the final analysis, however, it will probably be other teachers who provide the most frequent and effective coaching to encourage peers to master new techniques; therefore, teachers should be given the responsibility and the time for peer coaching.

Superintendents should understand that peer coaching, in the long run, may be the most cost-effective means of promoting mastery of new instructional practices. Judicious use of substitute teachers to release faculty to observe and confer may be the most effective means of introducing instructional innovations.

Focusing on teachers in need. The goal of differentiated pedagogy may be difficult to achieve. Some teachers may have little experience with subgrouping students based on learning readiness, although in some subjects, teachers generally group students according to their level of mastery and differentiate instruction accordingly (i.e., business education in secondary schools and reading instruction in elementary schools). In science courses, students are generally grouped for laboratory experiences, but this does not occur for all classes. Subgrouping students based on readiness may take time for some teachers to use effectively.

A notable impediment to subgrouping in secondary schools is the master schedule. The fixed length of time for classes often militates against effective subgrouping. In addition, the organization of many secondary textbooks and the perceived need of teachers to "cover the ground" and complete courses of study lead teachers to believe that they cannot take the time to allow students to work in groups. Teachers may need good models to observe subgrouping of students in various subject areas. Some teachers may need assistance in creating and using diagnostic tests to verify the current level of knowledge and skill of their students; they may also need specific training in how to manage subgroups of students for instruction and when to change the groups based on further diagnoses. The foregoing should not be understood to mean that there is no need for whole group instruction. If students are to work in subgroups, it may be most efficient to first present common information to the total group so that students have the same basis to begin their work.

The concept of cooperative learning has been successfully implemented at all levels of public school education (Johnson, Johnson, & Smith, 1991). The explicit expectations for students who engage in cooperative learning and the training they receive may help teachers understand and accept the concept of subgrouping.

Using shared decision making for differentiated pedagogy. The departmental organization in secondary schools can provide a forum for teachers to discuss issues around diagnostic teaching, assessment, and the general concept of differentiated pedagogy. Department chairpersons may need special training to assist them to lead these discussions. If department meetings can focus on instructional matters and a general diagnosis of the needs of students, teachers can mutually support one another to master the concepts of differentiated pedagogy.

In some high schools, interdisciplinary teams of teachers are organized to instruct a common group of students, and many opportunities are available to engage in shared planning for instruction. Teachers in interdisciplinary teams take responsibility for knowing each student as fully as possible and making decisions to address the learning needs of individual students. This type of environment contains the best possible conditions for differentiated pedagogy. Also, interdisciplinary teams often have the freedom to modify the daily schedule to accommodate the needs of students—the optimum condition for secondary teachers to implement differentiated pedagogy.

Middle schools that are organized into grade-level teams afford similar conditions, as are elementary schools that are organized by grade-level teams or in family groups. These teams also need flexible scheduling to maximize student outcomes.

To use the sophisticated concepts of differentiated pedagogy, teachers must have time for reflection, analysis of student learning, and planning for multiple teaching-learning strategies. Without time made available for these critical tasks, the goal of differentiated pedagogy will not be reached.

Creating the Climate for
Professional Development and Evaluation

The active collaboration of the superintendent, the board, union leadership, and principals is crucial for creating an ideal climate for professional development. Each of these parties has a role to play in creating expectations for excellence in the performance of professionals.

The Superintendent's and the Board's Commitments

Under the leadership of the superintendent, the board of education should make it a high priority to create a climate for improved professional performance and evaluation of employees. Such a climate begins with the superintendent convincing the board and the community to invest in creating a continuous professional growth environment for its employees. Both the board and the superintendent should make public their seriousness of purpose about evaluation and professional development through public statements, media releases, and most important, through policy development and implementation.

The strongest statement a board can make about its seriousness in creating a climate for effective evaluation and professional development is to set aside a percentage of its annual budget for that purpose. I believe that every board of education in the country should set aside a minimum of 1% of its annual budget to support professional development. Most school districts spend at least 75% of their budgets on personnel costs; it seems prudent to spend 1% more on continuing professional development and evaluation so that the professionals in the district can function at their highest levels, which would ensure high-quality instruction for all students.

The Union's Commitment

Full participation of unions in developing plans for the evaluation and professional growth of their members contributes to a positive climate for this to occur. Union leaders should join with the superintendent and the board in taking a public position to support the improved performance of their respective members. In this day and age, a union would be short-sighted not to take such a public posture. Unions demonstrate an enlightened position when they join in supporting the enhancement of the professional performance of their members (see Chapter 7).

The Principal's Commitment

Establishing a positive climate for personnel evaluation and continuing professional growth is as important at the school level as it is at the district level. The principal cultivates a positive climate for professional growth by including teachers in making decisions about school-based professional development activities.

As a school board holds the superintendent accountable for creating a district climate for effective evaluation and professional growth, the principal is held accountable for creating a similar climate at the school level. The superintendent must make this goal an explicit expectation for the principals as educational leaders. When this expectation is created and when there is follow-up to monitor and evaluate its implementation, such a climate will emerge.

SUMMARY

The superintendent as an educational leader has a major responsibility to oversee the development of a comprehensive evaluation system and professional development program for principals and teachers. The superintendent must see that newly appointed and veteran principals understand their roles as educational leaders at the school level and make appropriate professional development training available to them to implement their responsibilities. The superintendent must ensure that principals are evaluated with regard to the quality of educational leadership they exercise. The role of principal as educational leader is a necessary condition for the achievement of educational excellence, particularly with respect to the professional development of teachers.

The wise superintendent will make sure that principals and teachers understand what is expected of them and make appropriate resources and sufficient training available so they have the skills needed to fulfill the expectations. In the final analysis, principals and teachers must be evaluated on their respective roles to provide effective instruction and assessment for students.

Differentiated pedagogy is given as an example of teacher development. This diagnostic approach to instruction assists teachers to plan lessons based on the current level of their students' knowledge and skill.

A positive educational environment in a district is necessary for the improvement of instruction for students; to that end, commitments from the superintendent, the board, unions, the principals, and the teachers must occur to achieve the excellence agenda.

6

Community Involvement

As an educational leader, the superintendent is expected to build community support for the district's excellence agenda. To achieve this goal, he or she must involve all segments of the community. In this chapter, I describe my perspective of a superintendent's involvement with several constituencies: parents, businesses, community task forces, higher education institutions, senior citizens, and the political community. Forging and maintaining supportive relationships with these stakeholders is vital to the achievement of excellence in education. (See Chapter 11 for specific examples of community involvement.)

Parents as Partners

It seems trite to remind ourselves that parents are the first teachers of their children. The topic cannot be glossed over, however, when one reflects on the powerful influence of the formative years on subsequent schooling. Early childhood educators stress that each child needs to be ready for formal schooling when he or she reaches the appropriate legal age. Often, poor and minority parents need support to guide the development of school readiness in their children.

Parent Involvement

The ultimate goal for parents' involvement in their children's education is for the parents to understand, support, and collaborate with teachers; this requires close communication with one another. Parents need to understand and agree with the school's goals and have timely information regarding their children's progress.

School administrators must find creative ways to schedule the time for teachers and parents to discuss student progress. Arranging access for parents who lack transportation is another way school districts can help; in some districts, principals locate conference areas in housing communities and transport teachers there to make them more accessible for parents. Such accommodation communicates respect for parents who lack the resources to come to the school.

Programs that teach parents how to understand and deal with the growth and development cycles of childhood and adolescence help parents fulfill their responsibilities. Assisting parents to set up home study schedules for their children supports the goals that both schools and parents want.

Child Care Programs

Schools need to be sensitive to parents who require child care programs before and after school. The need for such arrangements are more likely to expand in future years. School leaders must be responsive to parents and help them fulfill these needs; administrators may have to cut the bureaucratic red tape to make space available in schools. School leaders' concerns about legal and insurance problems can be resolved through appropriate planning and oversight.

Children and youths need psychological security both at home and in school to be successful. The lack of stability in the home life of many children and adolescents today poses special problems for both the schools and parents. The provision of appropriate care before and after school may help with this basic psychological need.

Parent Volunteers

Parent volunteers are necessary to help teachers and principals provide for the needs of children and the school. Principals and teachers are responsible for creating a climate where parents are welcome. Unfortunately, some principals and teachers discourage parents from participating in school life.

In rare cases, parents can get involved in power struggles in parent organizations or volunteer groups. In such instances, principals should take swift, decisive action to solve the problems, thus minimizing the negative effect on the school. A principal may need help from central office administrators or individuals within the community to help resolve such problems.

Parents and School Governance

In the future, parents may have more voice in the control of their community's schools. In some districts, through site-based management patterns, parents participate in staffing and school regulation.

The Chicago school reform initiative is a case in point. The Illinois state legislature mandated a unique governance structure for schools in the city. Each school is now governed by a local community council made up of teachers, the principal, and parents—the majority are parents. The council has the authority to (a) hire the principal and teachers, (b) place the principal under a performance contract, (c) formulate school budgets, and (d) develop and implement policies and practices that give parents more direct involvement in their children's education.

The Chicago experiment was initiated by the city's business community and state legislature, who were frustrated in their attempts to make the Chicago schools more effective. The legislature's intent was based on the assumption that, by giving more control to the community, schools would be less bureaucratic, more responsive to the parents, and more effective. The long-range results of this change await future research and evaluation.

After several years of operation, the Consortium on Chicago School Research reported that approximately one third of the city's schools are functioning very effectively with site-based management, another third are struggling with governance issues, and the final third are still engaged in power struggles over who will control the schools (Bryck, 1993).

Site-Based Management

The current legal structure in most states leaves the sole responsibility for schools to the elected school board. Boards are generally not free to assign their legal responsibilities to local governance structures without appropriate action by state legislators. There is considerable interest in many state legislatures, however, in giving more autonomy to local agencies. The movement toward site-based management is likely to result in more involvement of parents and community members in school governance. Charter schools, for example, are gaining in popularity; typically, they give parents and community direct control over organization, governance, staffing, and educational issues. Superintendents and boards should examine how they can give more authority to schools for self-governance and still retain the legal rights of the board of education.

Superintendents and principals need to be aware that some community agencies and some adults may attempt to take over the schools; they do so to serve their own individual agendas and may not place the best interests of the children first.

The key to successful site-based governance of schools is adequate training for school personnel, parents, and community members in conducting effective meetings, consensus decision making, conflict resolution, budget development, and so on. The board and superintendent cannot assume that educators, parents, and community members will automatically be able to function effectively as a governing body. The lack of adequate training will produce the kind of mixed results that were described for the Chicago schools.

Business and Schools as Partners

Perhaps at no time in our nation's history has the opportunity for extensive involvement of business with the schools been greater than in the 1990s. Business leaders read the nation's demographics clearly. They perceive poor and minority populations growing at a faster rate than others. They recognize that the future workforce will come from this group of students, which the public schools have traditionally not served well. The business community is more willing than ever to support schools to improve the quality of its graduates.

What does business want from the schools? In my dealings with the business community, I found that they would like employees and work-study students who

follow directions and work well in groups;
possess strong interpersonal and communication skills (reading, writing, speaking, listening);

come to work on time, are regular in their attendance, and provide an
honest day's work;

have a positive attitude and work ethic; and

have the ability to solve problems related to the work environment.

The business community also wants schools to educate all children
effectively, especially those of average ability. If schools do their job well,
businesses will have to spend less time providing on-the-job or remedial
training for employees. Basically, business leaders want schools to be run
as efficient business enterprises.

Business leaders can be severe critics of schools, especially in urban
areas. The best way to overcome criticism is to get these leaders and their
associates directly involved in the schools. As an urban superintendent, I
found that some severe critics of public education within the business
community had never been inside a public school. Inviting them to become
involved and getting them into the schools did a great deal to convert these
leaders from critics to supporters.

Partnerships With Business

Achieving formal partnerships with businesses and industries takes a
great deal of effort. Successful partnerships require that the school district
and a business each assign responsibility to one individual to oversee
operations. Both entities must (a) give the responsible persons in the
partnership sufficient time to do the job, (b) allow time to develop trusting
relationships between business people and educators, and (c) gain commitments from both schools and businesses for provision of financial and
human resources to develop the partnership.

Here are some ways in which schools and businesses can engage in
productive partnerships:

Invite business leaders as speakers for classes or student assemblies.

Engage business people as tutors, mentors, and links with other community resources.

Involve business leaders in defining particular educational outcomes
in specific courses to bring schools and businesses together in
developing meaningful goals for students.

Use business leaders as advisers to improve the quality of the business
operations of a school district.

Seek business funding for specific educational programs or student activities.

Recruit business support for the development of new programs to prepare future workers for their businesses.

Once positive relationships have been developed, they cannot be taken for granted. It takes constant communication among the parties to maintain successful partnerships. School personnel must be responsive to their business counterparts and recognize and appreciate their contributions. Opportunities need to be created both in the business world and in the schools to affirm the accomplishments of the partnerships. (Chapter 11 provides specific examples of successful business-education partnerships.)

Community Task Forces

An important vehicle to engage the community with district professionals is the task force. The superintendent can create task forces to study problems, evaluate programs, or focus on educational planning (see Chapter 3). Stakeholders in task forces become knowledgeable about the district and committed to its excellence agenda.

Careful selection of community members to serve on task forces serves many purposes. Some will be selected because they (a) possess expertise that the district does not have, (b) can build networks of support for specific programs, (c) can make contact with other individuals and agencies to help the district meet its goals, (d) wield significant influence in the taxpayer community, or (e) are important members of the area's power structure.

My experience working with community task forces suggests that several cautions are in order. First, those invited to participate are likely to be busy people who will insist on efficient use of their time. Their full participation will depend on their perception of the task force as doing something important to which they can contribute. Second, meetings will have to start on time, be run efficiently, and be productive. Third, members need to know that their valuable time is going to result in a report or recommendations that will be seriously considered by the administration and the board; the superintendent and the district will lose credibility with these people if they think that their efforts are not going to be taken seriously. Publications that communicate the work of task forces and the implementation of results will help keep businesses' support; maintaining communication with these stakeholders tends to increase their willingness to serve in the future.

Rotating task force membership to engage other community members builds broad support for the district. Recognizing task force accomplishments by holding receptions when the work is completed builds goodwill and encourages continuing support.

Higher Education Institutions

Higher education personnel should be included on task forces for several important reasons. First, involvement of these faculty or administration members keeps them informed about the district's priorities and helps them identify ways their institutions can help.

Second, engagement of college and university faculty helps inform them about potential changes in teacher and administrator training programs to address the district's needs.

Third, such relationships foster effective student-teaching and internship experiences for prospective teachers. The roles of the school district and university personnel must be made clear and meet the needs of both parties. Expectations for student teachers and interns must be carefully spelled out, and the expectations for cooperating teachers, intern supervisors, and the college supervisors must be clearly understood. To the extent that these conditions are met, both the schools and the higher education institutions will have positive experiences.

Fourth, the presence of higher education personnel in district staff development programs provides benefits to both parties. Most school districts do not have all the technical expertise they need to plan or implement professional development programs and can use assistance from higher education institutions to meet their goals. Providing these expert services helps higher education personnel better understand how to modify advanced degree programs for practicing educators.

Fifth, some school districts do not have research or evaluation staff to study programs or identify needs. Higher education experts who can assist the school district in these areas make an important contribution. Successful evaluation requires that districts specify clearly what they need, when they need it, and in what form they need the data. Higher education personnel need to pay close attention to the school district's need for timely evaluative data and the desired format. Clearly written expectations for higher education personnel and the school district will most likely result in a positive experience for both institutions.

Involving Senior Citizens in the Schools

Senior citizens are an important constituency to engage actively in school affairs; they can be a great resource for the schools if effectively used. Many seniors have time and a great deal of talent to offer, if the schools take the time to involve them. Schools can build this relationship by contacting senior citizen organizations, who can identify talent that the district can use to enhance their educational programs.

School districts can build a database of senior citizens who have expertise, life experiences, or hobbies that could be used to help students. Seniors citizens can contribute their knowledge or skills directly or be a source of oral history for students. Seniors can contribute expertise that the school district may not have.

Intergenerational programs have demonstrated the benefits to individual seniors as a result of involvement in the schools. Often, it gives the senior citizen something important to do and look forward to and provides them with a great deal of satisfaction; contact with younger people can be a source of inspiration for senior citizens. Building intergenerational understanding is perhaps one of the most important results for students. These relationships can provide foster grandparents for children who may not have frequent (or any) contact with their own grandparents and also help children and youths to gain an understanding of the aging process. Senior-student programs help to build mutual respect, understanding, and compassion.

Constituency building for the school district is another important outcome of formally developed programs for senior citizens. In many communities, the number of senior citizens is growing at a rapid rate and can be an important voting block in local elections. If they view the schools positively, they may be more likely to be supportive when tax referenda or other important matters come up. If seniors feel no connectedness with the schools, they can develop negative attitudes. Because school districts use a large portion of a community's financial resources, senior citizen support continues to be a very important issue. School districts should take seriously the opportunity to include these important citizens in their ongoing activities.

The Political Community

School districts are political entities of state government. The majority of financial support for most school districts, however, comes from local taxes; state government, and, to some extent, the federal government (depending on the type of community) also fund local educational agencies. Political leaders can be important allies of school districts, and it is important for superintendents to build good relationships with local, state, and federal officials; at times, the superintendent will have to lobby legislators to gain financial support for the district.

In some communities, the school district is dependent on local government for the majority of its budget. In these circumstances, it is imperative that good working relationships are developed and maintained. In those instances where city government has direct control over expenditures of district funds (other than personnel costs), the lack of a positive working relationship can be severely detrimental.

Cooperation with politicians is a two-way street. Superintendents need the goodwill of politicians to gain the support needed for schools. Politicians, on the other hand, need to be responsive to their constituents to be reelected. Also, political leaders often need information to respond to inquiries from their constituents, and they are sometimes asked by their constituents to intervene regarding school matters and job opportunities in school districts. Superintendents can respond by inquiring into situations and providing requested information. Superintendents need to draw the lines of propriety carefully and clearly, however, with regard to job opportunities. A good stance for a superintendent is to provide opportunities for interviews on request by a politician but give no guarantees regarding outcomes. Most elected officials are satisfied with courtesies extended to them and their constituents. A few politicians may try to influence the superintendent to hire certain individuals. The best policy is not to succumb; if one does give in, there will be no end to the pressure. The superintendent who holds his or her ground regarding qualifications or competence will generally be respected by most politicians.

Fiscal Support for School Districts

State and local politicians need to be informed about the district's fiscal status and its financial needs. Even though a district may be independent of local and county government by having its own taxing authority, it is important to keep city and county officials informed of annual budget plans. Maintaining communication with area officials about revenue flow and potential future fiscal needs keeps all parties knowledgeable about financial issues that affect the same taxpayers.

It is also important for superintendents to maintain close contact with state representatives regarding school funding. Regular meetings concerning general plans for the school district help them respond intelligently to constituents about educational matters. Such meetings also inform the state representative of the financial status of the school district and indicate ways in which the state assembly can assist local funding of education. It is wise for the superintendent and associates to collaborate with local, state, and national elected officials to advance the cause of the school district specifically and public education in general.

Boards of Education as Political Entities

The governance structure of American schools is one of the most significant issues relating to the quality of education in America (Twentieth Century Fund, 1992). Boards of education across the nation are viewed as part of the problem of the lack of school effectiveness. This section explores, from the perspective of my experience, the role of the board as a political entity; in addition, I describe some of the general problems experienced by superintendents in dealing with board members.

Most boards of education for the more than 15,000 school districts across the nation are elected by citizens; in a few of the nation's cities, they are appointed by the mayor. In some communities, board members are elected at large to serve the total community; in others, members are elected by districts.

Board members elected by district have a tendency to be more constituent-oriented than those elected at large; they may need to reflect closely the values of their constituents if they are to be elected and reelected. These members may need to demonstrate that they have gained particular advantages for their districts to remain in office and, as a result, may strive to satisfy the needs of their own district and show less concern for other regions of the district.

Boards elected by district may not necessarily be problematic. As a superintendent, I have worked with boards both elected at large and by district. Some boards elected by district have acted as if they were elected at large—their concern for the entire school district far exceeded their concerns for the limited area they were elected to represent.

In my experience, board members who perceive election to the school board as a political stepping stone to city or state government typically tend to be constituent oriented. The political boundaries for school boards and city councils may be closely aligned. Board members who plan to seek higher political office may want to create a heightened public image so that the electorate is more aware of them; they will want to be noticed by the media, or they will take on issues that they believe will advance their image with their electorate.

Why People Run for Boards of Education

Most board members receive no compensation for their service. They tend to put in long hours of service on behalf of a school district. Why do citizens run for school boards? In my experience, citizens run for election to school boards to (a) offer public service, (b) improve the quality of education for children and youths, (c) promote a special interest in broadening programs for students, (d) ensure that the school district has adequate support to provide the best possible education for the children of the community, (e) monitor that the district is spending tax dollars wisely, (f) provide expertise to enhance the operations of the district, (g) improve the education of poor and minority children or special-needs students, and (h) ensure that the district appoints high-quality professionals to teaching and administrative positions.

Among the less idealistic reasons that motivate some citizens to run for boards of education are to (a) prevent a board from taking some proposed action (e.g., closing a school), (b) put forward a special interest (e.g., a right-wing agenda), (c) exert political patronage regarding employment, (d) fire a superintendent, (e) satisfy a need for power, and (f) get involved in the management operations of the district.

Obviously, this last group of reasons can cause superintendents and districts serious problems. One of the most serious issues is that of board members whose primary interests are to provide employment for friends, relatives, or political supporters; for such members, personal loyalty tends to be more important than the person's competence for a particular position.

Single-issue candidates, once elected to the board, can cause problems if they are unable to balance their special interest with the overall responsibility of being a board member. Among the single issues about which board members may lobby are (a) interscholastic sports, (b) vocational education, (c) special education, (d) sex education programs, (e) certain textbooks or curricula, (f) specific orientations to curricula (e.g., Afrocentric), and (g) particular values to be espoused in the curriculum.

Needless to say, board members who advance their own agenda can cause problems for other board members and for the superintendent. The superintendent will have to treat these board members with respect while making his or her position on important matters quite clear. More often than not, other board members or the board president can help deal with the single-issue board member and redefine his or her concerns in the perspective of the total responsibility of a board member. Most single-issue members quickly become overwhelmed as they deal with the broad range of issues that confront board members; although they may not lose interest in their agenda, they begin to see a much bigger picture of the district than they ever imagined.

Elected Boards of Education: Advantages and Disadvantages

The advantages of elected as opposed to appointed boards rest primarily in the fact that the members purportedly represent the people who elect them. Where state law empowers the mayor of a city to appoint the board, the members may feel obliged to advance the mayor's agenda for the school district rather than represent the views of parents.

Another advantage of an elected board is that it can become as diverse as the population it represents, particularly if elected by districts, fulfilling the notion of representative government. Citizens typically have more direct access to a publicly elected official than to one who is appointed.

Appointed boards of education, on the other hand, may not fully reflect the citizenry they serve. They may have an overrepresentation of business and professional people who do not necessarily share the interests of parents of children who attend public school. Boards appointed by blue-ribbon committees or by some form of the judiciary may be composed of persons judged to be competent to adequately reflect the higher interests of the community; the general citizenry, however, may perceive these boards to be elitist.

The Problem With School Boards

Whether elected or appointed, boards of education are viewed as a significant part of the problem of public education in America. Why is this so? The report of the Twentieth Century Fund Task Force on School Governance identified micromanaging by board members as the most significant problem facing school districts in America (Twentieth Century Fund, 1992).

Theoretically, boards are supposed to set priorities and policies that govern the operations of the school district and evaluate the extent to which they are achieved. The administration is charged to implement the policies and priorities of the board and run the schools. Some boards, however, want to become directly involved in the day-to-day operations of the school district. Some board members want to give direct orders to district employees who, fearing for their jobs, accede to these directives. Sometimes this can go on for a period of time without the knowledge of the superintendent. Some board members may go directly to a principal, for example, and insist that a student problem be resolved in a manner satisfactory to a parent or the board member. Others may put pressure on personnel departments to hire certain individuals. Some try to give orders to maintenance staff and to athletic coaches. The foregoing list is just a sample of the types of micromanagement in which some board members engage.

A serious aspect of micromanaging by board members is that superintendents often get caught in the cross-fire between board members and staff and, as a result, become very vulnerable. Board members attend national and state school board conventions, which include, among other activities, very popular sessions on "how to fire superintendents"; "how to hire superintendents" sessions are also popular. The life span of a superintendent in one community averages fewer than 6 years; in the large cities of the nation, the average span of a superintendent's service is fewer than 3 years. No wonder American education is in trouble! The constant turnover results in little being accomplished for students. For example, during the 12 years I was superintendent in Pittsburgh, Pennsylvania, many of the country's largest districts had as many as five superintendents. Without stable leadership, districts cannot hope to sustain initiatives long enough to see the benefits of improved education for students. It takes a minimum of 5 years, in my judgment, to mobilize action and achieve any significant results in a district; it takes a decade to institutionalize changes that can produce and sustain positive results for students.

The report of the Task Force on School Governance (Twentieth Century Fund, 1992) calls for the creation of local education policy boards to address the current problems with existing school boards. Involved in policy development and oversight, policy boards would focus on developing strategic plans for school systems with the major emphasis being accountability for results. The task force specifies that these boards not be involved directly in the business affairs of the district or in collective bargaining. Rather, they would oversee auditors to verify the implementation of their policies. Policy boards would hire only the top administrative positions in the district; the district administration would be responsible for all other hiring, informing the board of their decisions. For these conditions to become reality, a reexamination and rewriting of state statutes governing the operation of boards of education would be necessary, along with the reeducation of current board members and careful education of the educational policy board members.

The Twentieth Century Fund report recommends that, for city schools, the mayor appoint the school board based on recommendations from a broadly based screening panel. Such an arrangement would build better working relationships between city government and districts, and the needs of children and youths would be served more effectively. The task force recommends, as an interim step, that city school boards be composed of members elected both at large and by district, with the majority of members elected at large.

To address improved school governance, I propose a mixture of appointed and elected board members to serve all of the nation's schools. Appointed members should be recommended to a community's executive authority (e.g., mayor, town government) by a blue-ribbon screening committee; the town officials or the mayor *would be required to appoint only from a list of those recommended.* Other members would be elected at large rather than by district. The majority of the board would be appointed; thus, a nine-member board would have five appointed members and four members elected at large. Laws may have to be changed in some states to provide appropriate fiscal authority to a board that has a majority of appointed members. The board would also serve as an educational policy board as described by the task force report (Twentieth Century Fund, 1992). With the elected members representing the community at large, citizens could be reasonably assured that the interests of the entire community would be kept in mind. The appointed members could ensure that the broad racial and ethnic constituents of the community were represented, and they could be selected from the business and professional community, where the separation of policy and administration is more fully understood. The type of board described here is more likely to focus on policy development and leave the administration of the school district to the superintendent.

SUMMARY

The superintendent plays an important role in developing relationships in the community to gain and maintain support for the school district. He or she needs to oversee effective school relationships with parents, the most important stakeholders.

Parents can best support the schools by taking an active interest in their children's progress and maintain effective communication with teachers. Schools must provide a safe and psychologically secure environment for all children.

Emerging national demographics indicate that a majority of the future workforce will be made up of Hispanic and African American citizens. If the nation is to prosper economically, children and youths from these ethnic groups will have to take their rightful place as productive contributors to the economy.

The superintendent can engage parents, the business community, higher education institutions, and citizens to participate in task forces that will plan and help implement important initiatives for the school district. He or she needs to develop and maintain contact with elected officials to keep them informed of the district's progress and its needs. The legal framework that defines the relationship between the school district and local, regional, and state governments will determine the role that the superintendent must play.

The most significant political relationships a superintendent has are with members of the board of education. As elected officials, board members play a significant role in the development of policies that guide the school district. The superintendent must develop an effective working relationship with the board members, focus their time and attention on their role as policymakers, and enlist their support of the district's vision for excellence.

Citizens run for boards of education for a variety of reasons. A major problem facing American education is the tendency of board members to want to micromanage the district. A policy-oriented board is proposed as a means of overcoming this problem. It is recommended that a majority of all boards be composed of persons appointed by the executive authority of a community from a list compiled by a blue-ribbon committee; the other members would be elected at large.

Reform Initiatives
and Educational Leadership

7

Collaborating With Unions to Achieve Educational Reform

Educational reform in the 1990s requires extensive cooperation between unions, district administrations, and boards of education. Professional unions must move away from the narrow concerns of wages, hours, and conditions of employment if reform is to succeed. The agendas of teacher unions must evolve so that professionalism, accountability, and school effectiveness share equal billing with bread-and-butter issues. Superintendents and boards must also change to view professional unions as partners in educational reform and develop effective working relationships with them.

Professional unions are in a powerful position to mobilize their members to embrace and support educational reform; they can also pull the plug on reform. If unions are to support changes, they must perceive themselves as legitimate partners with administrators and boards; only then will educational reform become effective. The future viability of professional unions, in my judgment, will depend on their ability to work collaboratively with superintendents and boards to improve the results of schooling.

Professional unions need to create a public perception that they, too, are concerned with achieving educational excellence for the students in their respective communities.

Hill, Wise, and Shapiro (1989) identified six urban districts that achieved broadscale collaboration between unions, district management, and the business community to support educational reform. In another study, Kerchner and Koppich (1993) described how 10 urban and suburban school districts developed trust agreements between unions and management to achieve better educational outcomes for their students. The Pittsburgh, Pennsylvania, school district is cited in both studies.

This chapter discusses the collaboration between the Pittsburgh Federation of Teachers (PFT) and the Pittsburgh school administration during the 1980s and early 1990s. It describes the actions I took with the board of education and the presidents of the teachers' and administrators' unions to forge viable relationships and initiatives. The goals of both the union and the administration are noted, along with brief synopses of specific initiatives. Subsequent chapters in Part II describe more fully some Pittsburgh initiatives from their excellence agenda.

I'll begin the chapter by sketching out some of the conditions needed to bring about union-management cooperation in a school district and then tell the Pittsburgh story of union-management collaboration. Similar scenarios in Poway, California, and Greece, New York, are described in the final sections.

Trust: The Foundation of Collaboration

A common thread in the studies by Hill et al. (1989) and Kerchner and Koppich (1993) is that effective collaboration requires a climate of trust in which both school and labor leaders respect one another and appreciate each other's roles.

Trusting relationships are built between people who communicate frequently, are true to their word, and follow through on their promises to take action. The superintendent and the union leaders need to meet frequently for extended dialogue about the needs of the school district, the union, the administration, and the board. The superintendent and the union leaders need to collaborate successfully on small initiatives first, to achieve success that will build a sense of trust.

Building trusting relationships with union officials is particularly vital for a superintendent who comes from outside the district. If promoted from within the district, he or she is a "known commodity" and the development of trusting relationships might be easier. One cannot take anything for granted, however; trust needs to be earned and maintained over a long period of time.

Effective collaboration is built by leaders working together on tasks that are important to both parties. It is not enough for support staff members to work together; the superintendent and the union leaders themselves must take an active part in all joint undertakings to communicate that such collaboration is important.

The superintendent is responsible for designing and implementing a reform agenda with the full participation of the professional unions; such involvement of union leaders and members greatly increases the chances of successful implementation. Participation usually builds commitment, and union members can be influential in supporting change initiatives at the school level.

How to Build Cooperative Relationships

From my perspective, there are four aspects to building cooperative relationships between the superintendent and union leadership. First, the superintendent needs to recognize the legitimate needs of the union leaders and members. Addressing long-standing, unresolved issues may be an important way to move the relationship forward.

Second, the superintendent should recognize that teacher unions in the 1990s are likely to advocate for greater teacher responsibility and leadership. The American Federation of Teachers, for example, is interested in creating roles that enable teachers to influence educational reform without having to leave the ranks of teaching. The Pittsburgh Federation of Teachers was active in seeking leadership roles for the best teachers who could positively influence their peers and educational initiatives at the school level yet still teach children and youth. The superintendent will have to develop these new roles collaboratively with the administrators' union so that administrative leadership responsibilities are both protected and enhanced; this issue is of great importance to principals.

Third, the superintendent must present to the union leaders the positions, interests, and concerns of all the school board members. He or she may want to arrange informal meetings with the board and union leaders to help clarify issues and resolve misunderstandings. Informal meetings may help maintain positive working relationships between the unions, the administration, and the board.

Open and honest communication between the board and the unions can make the formal negotiations process more productive and efficient. Both parties know that a certain amount of posturing has to take place during formal collective bargaining so that union members see their leaders supporting their causes. When a good working relationship exists, however, informal exchanges away from the bargaining table can greatly facilitate acceptable agreements. Trust and positive informal relations between the parties tend to eradicate the confrontational nature of traditional collective bargaining.

Fourth, teams of administrators and teachers formed to address issues of mutual concern can help develop a positive work climate. For example, the PFT and the administration created the Burdensome Paperwork Committee to address the issue of excessive paperwork for teachers; a similar task force was created with the Pittsburgh Administrators Association (PAA). These committees, composed of central administrators and teachers or administrators, identified ways in which redundant or unnecessary paperwork could be eliminated and clerical work streamlined to ease the burden on building-level personnel. The important by-products of such task forces are more effective working relationships and greater trust among teachers, principals, and central office administrators.

Union and Management Collaboration in Pittsburgh

From the perspective of union-management relations in general, the Pittsburgh region has a unique place in American economic history. From the days of the Homestead Steel strike, unions were active in seeking improved wages, hours, and working conditions for their membership. Given the history and strong labor climate in Pittsburgh, it is not surprising that the PFT became an effective voice for its members. It is the largest of the unions in the school district and sets the pace for negotiations for other unions. Because of its size and the effectiveness of its full-time leadership, it is a strong force in the school district. The PAA, in comparison, has a much smaller membership and does not have full-time leadership; as a result, it does not enjoy the same stature as the PFT.

Collaboration With the PFT

In 1982, the first of many compromises was made that characterized the spirit of collaboration between the administration and the PFT. I directed the staff development team to plan a summer school program in which the principals would be the teachers, as part of the professional development program for principals (see Chapter 10 for details). When the PFT president heard of these plans, he wanted me to clearly understand that "teachers teach, principals don't teach." After a lengthy conversation, I persuaded him that it would be in the union's best interests to support this initiative; it would communicate to the general public a serious commitment to improving the quality of education. I then proposed adding an afternoon session for students, offering instruction in the arts and in recreation, which PFT members would teach. This compromise exemplified the relationship between the administration and the teachers' union that helped set the stage for progress in the Pittsburgh public schools during my tenure.

Collaboration in School Closings and Subsequent Reopenings

One of the priorities voted by the Pittsburgh Board of Education in 1981 was the management of enrollment decline. This meant that schools had to be closed. In 1970, the district had approximately 70,000 students; by 1980, the number had declined to 47,000 students. Enrollment projections indicated that by 1990 the district would have 35,000 students and then begin to increase. Few schools had been closed since 1970 to deal with the problem of decline; the board voted in 1981 to have me address it. Closing schools would pose a problem for everyone; the PFT could foresee significant layoffs of teachers.

High School Closings

School enrollment clearly indicated that the city had too many high schools. The seating capacity of the 14 schools could accommodate 25,000 students; there were 18,000 students enrolled and projections indicated that by 1990 there would be only 11,000. The plan ultimately adopted by the board included the closing of two secondary schools and the conversion of another into a special program school.

Union and Management Collaboration at Schenley High

One of the candidates for closing was Schenley High School. It had a capacity of 1,600 students yet it enrolled only half that number. I proposed to the board that Schenley be retained as a conventional school and that the unused space be converted to a teacher center to house an intensive staff development program for high school teachers. The Schenley High School Teacher Center is described in Chapter 10; the full cooperation of the PFT was needed to achieve this goal.

The PFT worked with the administration in helping to allay the fears of teachers who would be displaced or furloughed by the closings. Both parties agreed that these teachers would be part of the replacement teacher pool for the Teacher Center (see Chapter 10). The PFT leadership cooperated in the planning of the Teacher Center and the recruitment of its faculty. Their support was vital to achieving the goals established for the Center.

This cooperative venture served the purposes of both the administration and the PFT. The administration could point to the Center as a direct effort to improve the quality of education for students and the quality of personnel evaluation in secondary schools. The PFT could point to its cooperation as a serious gesture to improve the quality of education for students. Both parties benefited from the public perception of a district determined to improve the quality of education for its youth. It was clearly a "win-win" situation.

Continued Collaboration at
Brookline and Greenway Schools

The model of collaboration that established the Schenley High School Teacher Center was used to establish teacher centers for the elementary and middle school levels. The Brookline Elementary School Teacher Center and the Greenway Middle School Teacher Center followed the same pattern of collaboration regarding school closing and reopening as at Schenley.

Another important collaborative issue emerged with the new centers. One of the most costly features of the Schenley Center was that of replacement teachers used to release regular teachers from their classrooms to attend the Center program.

Because both the PFT and the administration were pleased with the results of the Schenley Center, I approached the PFT president about using a provision in its contract to help support the elementary and middle school centers. The contract called for 50 school-based spare teachers at the opening of every school year. These permanent substitute teachers were assigned to large schools throughout the district to be used on a daily basis as the first line of substitute teachers. The PFT president agreed to assign these teachers to the teacher centers so that the district would be spared the additional cost of replacement teachers. Because of this collaboration, it became fiscally possible to open teacher centers at the elementary and middle school levels.

Collaboration at Fulton

Fulton Elementary School was closed; it was reopened as the Fulton Academy for Geographic and Life Sciences. Here lies an interesting story of collaboration. Fulton Elementary School faced problems that affected its reputation in its neighborhood; white parents in the neighborhood elected to send their children to the district's magnet school system as a means of escaping a school they perceived as ineffective. The PFT agreed to work with the administration to close the school, restaff it with new teachers and administration, and reopen it as a Geographic and Life Sciences Academy. The district collaborated with the National Geographic Society, the neighboring Pittsburgh Zoo, and the Carnegie Institute to plan a thematic program that would attract neighborhood families back to their school.

Before the school was reopened, it was deluged with requests from white parents wanting their children to return to their neighborhood school. The resultant overcrowding caused the district to reopen a closed school a mile away from Fulton, as an adjunctive campus to handle the large number of students who wanted to attend. The school opened successfully and the parents became very active in working to maintain and improve the quality of education for their children. Fulton exemplifies the positive results of collaboration with the PFT: The school was revitalized, the parents enrolled their children in their neighborhood school, and the faculty developed an exciting and interesting program with local and national organizations.

These outcomes were achieved because an enlightened union leadership collaborated with a superintendent, board, and administration. These examples illustrate the general spirit of cooperation that set the stage for even more dramatic collaboration for educational progress.

Landmark Negotiations With the PFT

Between 1980 and 1985, substantial progress was made in changing the climate for public education in Pittsburgh. Collaboration between the administration, the PFT, and the PAA resulted in the creation and implementation of numerous initiatives to improve the quality of education. A spirit of optimism for public education began to pervade the city. One board of education member suggested to the president and me, in the summer of 1985, that many of the parents in his district were thinking about returning their children from private to public schools. The parents were concerned, however, about a possible teachers' strike. A lengthy strike in 1967 was still on the minds of parents. The board member suggested that if the district could reach an early settlement with the teachers, it would help parents finalize their decision to return their children to public schools.

The board president, the board labor counsel, and I met privately with the PFT president and counsel to explore the possibility of an early settlement. The strategy was to focus on settling the economic issues quickly. To avoid lengthy negotiations about educational or administrative matters, this group proposed an educational forum where the administration and the PFT could meet on a predetermined agenda. The goal was to discuss educational matters away from the bargaining table; if agreements could be reached, they would be presented to the board and the PFT membership for approval. After ratification by both parties, the agreements would be added to the subsequent contract—this process represents the concept of a trust agreement as cited by Kerchner and Koppich (1993). The PFT agreed to this proposal, and in a short time, agreement was reached on the financial package and the contract was settled before the opening of school.

The Teacher Professionalism Project

The teacher professionalism project (TPP) was created as the forum for continuing discussion on educational issues. The early bird settlement confirmed a spirit of optimism in the city about public education and was seen as a sign of labor peace that helped solidify the growing confidence in the public schools. The TPP was part of the negotiated agreement to engage in discussion around topics of interest to the PFT and the administration.

The instructional cabinet, an important element of the TPP, became an effective instrument for the involvement of teachers in educational improvement. In effect, each school's cabinet became the governance structure for its educational matters (Wallace, Radvak-Shovlin, Piscolish, & LeMahieu, 1990). The purpose of the cabinets was to engage teachers and principals in discussion and shared decision making about matters of instruction and, thereby, improve the quality of education for students. During the first year of the TPP, cabinets were formalized and training in shared decision making was given to teachers and principals.

From 1985 to 1988, the TPP continued to grow and develop in dealing with important educational issues. Teacher professionalism was clearly an important issue for the entire school district. The PFT and the administration each designated members to sit on the steering committee of TPP. The administration team included the president of the PAA, principals, and central office administrators I designated. The PFT team comprised officers of the union and selected building representatives.

In 1988, the second consecutive early bird settlement was reached with the PFT, a year ahead of the contract expiration date. Again, financial matters were settled first.

Professionalism and Education Partnership

The TPP was expanded to specifically include the PAA as a full partner and was renamed the professionalism and education partnership (PEP). PEP was another evolutionary step in the effective collaboration between management and labor. The board, the PFT, the PAA, and the administration formally signed to confirm this important agenda. The clear goal of the partnership was to improve the quality of education for children and youths while simultaneously improving the quality of professional life for teachers and administrators. The PEP agreement capped the progressive collaboration that began with the needs assessment of 1980.

The Instructional Teacher Leader

One of the key features of PEP was the formalization of the role of instructional teacher leaders (ITL), who take part in the governance of the school in four ways:

1. Along with the principal as members of the instructional cabinet, they make decisions about the teaching program of the school.
2. They serve as a communication link between teachers in their department, team, or grade level and the principal.
3. They demonstrate pedagogical techniques and provide information about instructional trends.
4. They participate in the formative evaluation of teachers by observing and giving feedback to improve instruction, and they contribute to the principal's final rating of teachers.

The ITL evolved from the clinical resident teacher role established in the Schenley High School Teacher Center in 1983. The ITLs played an important role in the governance of the school and collaborated with the principal to improve the quality of education. They were nominated by their peers and selected by the principal. An internal certification procedure was developed in collaboration with the PFT. ITLs would receive formal training in observing and conferring from the staff development specialists. Following the training, they would demonstrate these abilities with peers for a panel composed of clinical resident teachers from the teacher centers, a principal, and a supervisor. If they demonstrated the capacity to effectively observe and confer, they were formally certified as ITLs; following certification, they received a stipend and were expected to carry out the four responsibilities described.

The ITL program served important purposes for both the PFT and the administration. The PFT viewed the program as providing teachers with an opportunity to exert leadership in instruction in the schools without having to leave the classroom to become an administrator. The administration viewed it as helping principals with quality control for instruction and in the teacher evaluation process.

The evaluative role of the ITL was always a problem for the PFT and its members. The position of the administration was that the principals had the legal responsibility for teacher evaluation; the ITLs were to collaborate with principals in observing and conferring with teachers to improve instruction. The role of the ITLs expanded quickly during the latter half of the 1980s—an extension of the duties of the existing department chair in the secondary schools and the team leader in the middle schools. It was a new role for elementary teachers.

The board's primary interest in the ITLs was the participation in teacher evaluation. The board insisted on annual evidence that ITLs had participated in giving any unsatisfactory ratings for teachers. The board was concerned about the cost of the ITL program because stipends and released time increased significantly over prior costs of department heads and team leaders.

Collaboration on Focused Teachers

Dealing with marginally competent or incompetent teachers is a task that has to be dealt with forthrightly; many school districts do not deal with this issue effectively. Yet to achieve excellence, marginal teachers must become competent and those who cannot reach the expected level of competence must be discharged. Pennsylvania school law is very explicit regarding teacher evaluation and dismissal. If a teacher receives two consecutive unsatisfactory ratings, he or she is automatically dismissed. With personnel evaluation the second highest priority identified by the Pittsburgh Board of Education in 1980, teacher and administrator evaluation received a great deal of attention.

Following formal training to observe and confer with teachers, principals were expected to deal with teacher competence—an explicit expectation of the superintendent and the board. The ITLs were expected to participate in teacher evaluations with the principals. The administration and the PFT developed a collaborative plan to deal with what were called *focused teachers:* teachers in danger of receiving an unsatisfactory rating. The goal of the program was to offer appropriate help so that they could become competent.

The plan for focused teachers included the following five elements:

1. A clear delineation of teacher deficiencies
2. The development of individual improvement plans
3. The identification of help to be provided by principals, supervisors, ITLs, and other relevant personnel
4. Specific actions to be taken by the teacher for self-improvement
5. A signed agreement for improvement

One school year was the usual time frame for improvement. If the teacher improved during that time, a satisfactory rating would be given; if no improvement was made, an unsatisfactory rating would be given, and the teacher would be headed for dismissal. In general, those teachers who took a positive attitude toward improvement and responded to help were successful. Those teachers who demonstrated a negative attitude and refused help did not improve; they were counseled to resign or were terminated. The focused teacher program provided a common meeting ground where the administration and the PFT collaborated to promote quality instruction for students in Pittsburgh.

School Restructuring

The collaboration of the 1980s resulted in another early bird settlement in 1991. Once again, a formal agreement with the PFT paved the way for its full participation in the design and implementation of school improvement. A school restructuring was initiated to give teachers and principals greater autonomy to design and implement programs.

Outcomes of Collaboration With the PFT

The collaborative relationship with the PFT during the 1980s into the early 1990s produced a high degree of teacher professionalism in the district. Student achievement increased significantly and many new educational initiatives were implemented to improve the quality of education for students. Teachers and administrators were intensely involved in many educational improvements that were reflected in the priorities set by the board of education in 1981, 1986, and 1991. Teachers believed that they could make a difference in their classrooms, their schools, and in their professional lives. A tremendous amount of creative energy was poured into educational programs that are described in subsequent chapters.

Open communication with the PFT was the norm during the 1980s. This is not to say that there were not some serious disagreements along the way. But where roadblocks were encountered, compromises were reached and the reform agenda moved forward. The most important product of collaboration clearly was the enhanced sense of empowerment and professionalism in teachers and administrators. Their joint work produced a variety of programs for students and professionals that won national recognition for the Pittsburgh public schools. Some of these award-winning programs will be described in the remaining chapters of this book.

Collaboration With the PAA

Under Pennsylvania law, the PAA, representing the more than 300 district administrators, has the right to meet and discuss terms and conditions of employment with the board of education. It does not have the right, however, to engage in collective bargaining per se. The law requires the board to meet with administrators directly, and the resulting agreements are published as public record. Several collaborations were undertaken during my tenure as superintendent.

Role Guides

The PAA's first collaborative endeavor was to revise the role guides for administrative positions to reflect the educational priorities set by the board in 1981. The role of principal, for example, was changed to emphasize educational and instructional leadership. Role guides, one part of the evaluation system for administrators, stated specific expectations across the range of administrative responsibilities. Each administrator was required to develop an annual plan to achieve particular outcomes reflecting the district's priorities for that year.

Salary Structures and Work Schedules

Second, I worked with PAA committees to develop a new salary structure and work year schedule for administrators to address past inequities; although it was impossible to remedy all inequities, substantial progress was achieved. The new work year and salary structure for school-based administrators was founded on the following: the teachers' work year, time to prepare for the opening and closing of school, 10 days for staff development training, and a differentiated length of school year depending on the level of schooling and the size of the school.

Staff Development

The third area of collaboration focused on a staff development program for principals as educational leaders. A task force composed of administrators and teachers addressed the priority of improving personnel evaluation. The board adopted the proposed plan, which was designed to prepare principals to be instructional leaders and to evaluate teachers more effectively. Chapter 10 describes the program in more detail.

Summer Academies

A fourth effort was the implementation of summer academies for principals, which began in 1982. Each summer thereafter, these academies offered continuing professional development as educational leaders. The participation of the administrators in planning the academies contributed, in large measure, to their success (see Chapter 10).

The PAA was supportive of collaborative efforts with the central office administration and participated fully in initiatives that involved the PFT. Jointly, both groups contributed significantly to the design and implementation of an agenda to provide a high quality of excellence in education for the students of Pittsburgh.

Outcomes of Collaboration With the PAA

Principals and central office administrators worked very hard to implement initiatives designed to achieve the priorities of the board of education. As a result, student achievement increased significantly and a multitude of new programs were implemented to improve the quality of education for children and youths. The administrators gained an increased sense of professionalism and a greater sense of pride in being in the city schools. As the district's agenda developed over the decade, principals and other administrators had many opportunities to make presentations at national conferences to describe programs that had emerged for the district. Programs such as the teacher centers brought hundreds of visitors from all over the country to see firsthand what was being done. These events helped to create a sense of a progressive district. And administrators enjoyed being part of a district that was perceived positively.

The collaborative efforts also created high expectations for administrators and increased their burden. Often, the cry was heard, "No more new programs!" Yet as a group, they responded very well to the pressure to perform. A researcher from the University of Pittsburgh evaluated some programs for the district; she uncovered a phenomenon that she labeled *the equity of pressure.* She told of her visits to schools throughout the district, where she found everyone—from the superintendent to the teachers—feeling pressure to perform (Salmon-Cox, 1983). This equity of pressure, she believed, helped account for the amount of innovation that she observed in the district. Pittsburgh administrators gave enormously creative, effective, and loyal service to the district.

Union and Management Collaboration in Suburban School Districts

Poway, California, a suburb of San Diego, and Greece, New York, a suburb of Rochester, are two suburban school districts that have developed exemplary models of collaborative educational reform accomplished through effective cooperation between unions, administration, and boards. As in Pittsburgh, the superintendents in both districts worked effectively with union leaders to bring about significant changes in the climate that moved the districts to extensive collaboration for educational reform. These accomplishments were made possible through trust agreements that existed outside the formally negotiated contracts in each district (Kerchner & Koppich, 1993).

Poway (California) Unified School District

Reform in the Poway Unified School District occurred for three reasons: a major influx of families with children in school, California's school reform legislation regarding mentor teachers, and a long history of union-management tension at the beginning of each school year.

The Poway district adopted and expanded the concept of peer review, originally developed in Toledo, Ohio, into "what is arguably the country's most fully developed peer review program" (Kerchner & Koppich, 1993, p. 166). Between 1975 and 1990, the district more than doubled its student population. Its need to integrate many new teachers each year during that period stimulated the development in 1987 of the Poway Professional Assistance Program for novice teachers. In 1990, the district developed a permanent teachers intervention program and an alternative evaluation program for experienced teachers. Most recently, the district has implemented a professional development program. The major teacher initiatives described here all operate in a shared governance structure under the trust agreement.

Novice Teacher Program

In 1987, to implement the novice teacher program, three teachers were designated as *teacher consultants* and released from full-time teaching positions for a 3-year term. Novice teachers were assigned to a teacher consultant and received assistance in setting up classrooms, preparing lesson plans, establishing discipline, and developing effective classroom routines. This support came early, was nonjudgmental, and helped shape and develop their skills. The consultant and the novice worked together about 40 hours during the crucial first year.

Mentor teachers receive a $4,000 annual stipend funded by the state, which designated this program a priority. About 5% of Poway teachers have been mentors at different times. All of the 350 new teachers brought into the district from 1985 to 1994 are still employed there and many have become mentor teachers (D. Raczka, personal communication, December 4, 1994).

The five-member board that oversees the project is composed of teachers appointed by the union and administrators appointed by the superintendent. Consultant teachers send reports to the board about the teachers they supervise and make recommendations to the superintendent and the school board regarding the continued employment of novices.

Permanent Teachers Intervention Program

In 1990, an intervention program was established to help tenured teachers. After receiving an unsatisfactory rating from an administrator, a tenured teacher could ask for assistance. On receiving a second unsatisfactory rating, intervention became mandatory. Reports to the school board by consultant teachers can become a part of a teacher's personnel file and be used as evidence in case of dismissal proceedings.

Alternative Evaluation Program for Experienced Teachers

The alternative evaluation program began in 1990. It allows teachers with 5 or more years of experience, with the approval of the site administrator, to request participation in the alternative evaluation program rather than the conventional one.

Under this program, a teacher develops goal statements focusing on professional development. A teacher-principal meeting is held early in the fall to reach agreement on the goals and on the criteria to be used for evaluation. Portfolio assessment, classroom action research projects, structured staff development, and peer assistance are some of the alternative evaluation criteria used. The principal and the teachers meet twice a year, and each teacher receives an administrator's summary evaluation at the end of the school year (Kerchner & Koppich, 1993).

Professional Development Program

The most recent initiative regards professional development for teachers. Rather than having a parade of workshops, the focus is on systematic professional development geared to educational improvement. At this time, there are no professional development programs for principals. The realization has emerged in the district, however, that everyone is accountable for student achievement: union, teachers, and administration.

Greece (New York) Central School District

In the 1980s, the Greece Central School District moved through three phases of reform in labor relations. The first was characterized by conflict and confrontation; the second phase was a period of building trust and experimentation. Much progress was made during the third phase in testing, refining, and institutionalizing educational reform (Kerchner & Koppich, 1993).

Following the 1987 to 1989 agreement with the Greece Teachers Association (GTA), two major steps were made toward reform. The first was the Council for Change, a joint committee of the board and the GTA, which was organized through negotiations to promote change throughout the district. New goals for the GTA emerged through this council. The combined efforts of teachers, council, board, PTA, and administrators resulted in the second major step, the GTA Renewal Plan. This reform document called for increasing shared decision making by teachers, both at the school and district level.

The School of Choice

One major reform initiative was the establishment of a *school of choice*. By 1990, enrollment increases resulted in reopening the West Ridge School, previously closed due to declining enrollments. The district seized on this opportunity for collaboration. Designed as a school of choice, staff members and students were chosen from volunteers. Teachers were asked to devote a year of planning prior to transferring to the new school and the group included parents who were willing to commit themselves and their children to the new school. A support team of other teachers, administrators, community representatives, and University of Rochester faculty members provided technical assistance.

The core planning team determined that all staff should share a common vision of the school and its mission. To achieve that shared vision, the team reached its own consensus of vision; from this, requirements for a new principal and for teachers emerged. Teacher applicants had to present a written statement of vision for a school of the future. A strong shared vision emerged as newly hired staff became involved in the next staff additions. The school's program included new instructional technology, extensive computer facilities, and strong parental involvement in instruction as well as in overall operations; all these ensured success in this multigrade, team-taught school (Kerchner & Koppich, 1993).

An addition to the West Ridge School doubled its size. The developer and the superintendent agreed to a school of the future whereby the developer built additional space at no cost to the district; space in that part of the building is leased to various agencies, such as senior citizen groups and day care centers, that must follow the district's basic curriculum. The school district has the right to determine who can lease space. In 30 years, when the developer has realized a sufficient return on the investment, the school addition will be donated to the district. West Ridge School has been recognized by the National Education Association (NEA) as an NEA Learning Laboratory. The district showcase, it is the result of collaborative decision making that was outside the conventional collective bargaining structure—another example of success built on a trust agreement (D. Pratt, personal communication, January 20, 1995).

A second elementary school of choice, Pinebrook School, has since opened; in addition, the district has a secondary school of choice that houses middle school and high school students.

Site-Based Management

Another major initiative was the implementation of site-based management, which emerged from the Shared Decision Making Advisory Council. With site-based management, Greece decentralized the district administration, resulting in approximately a 60% reduction in central office staff. Site-based management has had two important effects on the district: school-based budgeting and school-based problem solving.

Each school now prepares its own budget and determines how funds will be allocated; budgets provide for carryover funding and forward funding. In addition, 5-year budgets enable the schools to use money more wisely.

On the basis of successful site-based management, problem-solving facilitators have been trained in conflict management. When a problem occurs within a school, a facilitator enters discussions and the parties try to resolve the problem. If the problem solvers are unable to achieve resolution, they file their fact-finding report with the superintendent and union president. The superintendent and the union president may hand down a decision, much as an arbitrator would do. Under this conflict management program, only one grievance has been filed since 1988.

Collective Bargaining

A new approach to collective bargaining has resulted in several *perpetual contracts:* permanent contracts without a termination date that include broad statements of principle. The teachers' contract, although not a perpetual agreement, includes detailed language about teaching responsibilities. As of early 1995, negotiations were underway for an agreement to succeed the contract that expired in June 1994.

The Greece school district made great strides in educational reform through the collaboration of a risk-taking, empowering board, a divergently thinking superintendent, and a teachers union that chose to be treated as a professional organization. The current board is fiscally conservative and less risk taking; however, the reform agenda continues to move forward. With changes in board membership and a new superintendent, positive relations remain between the board, administration, union, and teachers.

Greece is one of largest suburban districts in New York state, with 21 schools accommodating 14,000 students. Educational reforms have had an important positive effect on the district. Significant reform has been achieved because superintendents and union leaders decided to collaborate for the benefit of students.

SUMMARY

Superintendents, boards, and union leaders must collaborate effectively to achieve school reform. Successful urban districts build effective working relationships with unions within the district and with business and community leaders outside the district to support reform.

The superintendent must build trusting relationships with union leaders to accomplish change. To build trust, the superintendent must (a) respect the legitimate needs of union leaders, (b) be open and honest in dealing with them, (c) recognize the emerging need for teachers to become involved in leadership and governance, and (d) continually communicate the board's interests.

School districts that build effective working relationships with unions develop trust agreements outside of contract negotiations. These parties engage in extended dialogue and reach agreement on educational matters, which later are adopted into contract language.

The collaboration with unions in Pittsburgh is reported in both the RAND and the Kerchner and Koppich studies. The Pittsburgh Federation of Teachers (PFT) collaborated extensively with me and the board in a variety of ways, which are shown in the Schenley, Brookline, and Greenway Teacher Centers, where the union agreed to close, reopen, and restaff the schools.

Three early bird contract settlements with the PFT produced the teacher professionalism project, the professionalism and education partnership, and school restructuring. These educationally oriented forums enhanced professionalism and paved the way for the development of instructional cabinets, instructional teacher leaders, and the focused teacher program.

Collaboration with the Pittsburgh Administrators Association (PAA) resulted in the partial solution of long-standing problems with wages and length of the work year. The PAA joined with the administration, the board, and the PFT to support academies for principals to enhance the quality of professional life for themselves and improve the quality of education for the children and youths of the district.

Exemplary collaborative relationships between administration and teacher unions in Poway, California, and Greece, New York, illustrate what can be accomplished when these parties work together. In Poway, the change in negotiating climate led to the development of trust agreements that increased teacher professionalism. Poway's novice teacher program, permanent teacher intervention program, alternative evaluation program, and professional development program grew out of a new spirit of collaboration. In Greece, a similar spirit led to the development of trust agreements that in turn led to the implementation of schools of choice and extensive involvement of teachers in site-based management.

8

Using Data to Guide
Educational Leadership

Data-oriented educational leadership begins with the analysis of qualitative and quantitative data obtained through needs assessment surveys, as discussed in Chapter 3. My belief is that educational leadership is most effective when (a) it starts with a full understanding of the status quo of a school district; (b) the superintendent uses both formative and summative evaluations to make decisions about program effectiveness; and (c) data are also used to make decisions about modifying, expanding, or terminating current initiatives or designing new ones to fulfill the district's needs.

In this chapter, I describe instances of data-based educational leadership in Pittsburgh, Pennsylvania, and Providence, Rhode Island, that are quite different from one another in their origins. Both initiatives (a) were

---

The summary of the 10 key issues and the information concerning 10 of the 39 specific recommendations presented in the Providence Blueprint for Education (PROBE) Commission Report, May, 1993, are used by permission of the Public Information Fund, Providence, RI.

developed in climates of dissatisfaction with public education in their respective communities, (b) used data analyses to guide educational change, and (c) created and implemented several educational programs designed to address the needs identified through data analysis.

In Pittsburgh, data-oriented leadership began when I became superintendent in 1980; I needed sound data to identify conditions needing improvement and initiated a needs assessment survey. My data-oriented leadership can be traced through my superintendency to retirement in 1992. Let me note here that the Pittsburgh Public Schools enjoy fiscal independence: The district levies property and other taxes, as specified in state law, and is relatively independent of city government.

In Providence, data-oriented leadership began with the Public Education Fund (PEF), a nationwide network of nonprofit organizations that broker relationships between schools and private funding sources, such as business. The local PEF sought to identify conditions that needed to be improved in the school district. An effort called the Providence Blueprint for Education (PROBE) provided data that helped identify the needs of the schools based on a survey of stakeholders in the district. A new Providence superintendent has used the PROBE data since 1992 to guide educational improvement. The Providence Public Schools depend on the mayor and the city government for local funding and fiscal operations; the mayor also appoints the school board, and city council must approve school district expenditures.

There are three major differences between Pittsburgh and Providence: (a) the institutions seeking the data to define the educational improvement effort, (b) the macro- and micropolitical conditions that define the school districts and circumscribe the change efforts, and (c) the financial resources available. A discussion follows regarding how these conditions impinged on the implementation of data-oriented educational leadership.

The Pittsburgh Story

In the fall of 1979, five new board of education members were elected in Pittsburgh; this board was determined to improve the quality of education for students and implement a desegregation plan devised by the district's staff. Of particular concern was the perceived lack of quality of education for many of the city's African American youth. In the spring of 1980, the board decided that a change in superintendent was needed; I was appointed and took office in September 1980.

1980 Through 1985

Needs Assessment Survey: September Through December 1980

The board's desegregation plan was successfully implemented in September 1980, even though it was challenged in court by a group of citizens; the challenge was based on the perception that the board plan did not go far enough in integrating the city's schools. The court decision, rendered in the spring of 1982, called for modifications to the earlier plan. The board was determined to turn the school district around at virtually any cost. Their concerns were multiple but unfocused.

Shortly after my arrival, I visited Professor William Cooley of the Learning Research and Development Center at the University of Pittsburgh and requested his assistance in designing and conducting a needs assessment survey. I needed help because I did not have an in-house evaluation staff, my early observations in the district and the city indicated that the concerns of persons inside and outside of the school district were extremely diverse, and my success in leading the district depended on gaining consensus on priorities. Cooley responded positively—my proposal was consistent with his studies of the use of data for decision making in the Pittsburgh schools.

Planning for the survey began in October 1980. Cooley and Bickel (1986) describe its purpose:

> The general objective was to identify conditions that can and should be improved. That is, the focus of the assessment was on identifying problems and solutions that were within the realm of the district's ability to influence and implement. In this way, the results were to be a basis for immediate local action. (p. 183)

A 30-member task force, half from the district's staff and half from the community, defined the scope of the survey and collected initial data on the members' concerns about the school district. The task force used the following five-step process:

1. Subcommittees were formed to deal with various areas that would be included in the survey.
2. Long lists of questions were developed by the subcommittees for potential inclusion in the survey.

3. Cooley and his colleagues organized these questions into survey instruments and pilot tested them with the client populations.
4. The task force reconvened to review the survey instruments and the procedures to be used in conducting the survey; the task force gave its approval.
5. The survey was administered in December 1980.

The survey instruments are described as follows by Cooley and Bickel (1986):

> Survey questions were of three general types: ratings on a 5-point scale that tried to establish the perceived seriousness of the problem (teacher absenteeism); rank orderings of conditions that could and should be improved (lack of instructional leadership on the part of building administrators); and open-ended questions (What is the most unsatisfactory part of your job?). (p. 185)

Four different instruments were developed and mailed to the following constituents: (a) building administrators, central staff, and counselors; (b) nurses, social workers, and psychologists; (c) paraprofessionals, clerical, custodial, and general staff; and (d) teachers.

In addition to the mailed surveys, structured interviews were conducted with board members and business and community leaders. Focused group interviews were held with secondary school students. Telephone surveys were conducted with households with public school children, private school children, and with no children in school. Thus, data were collected from a broad range of stakeholder groups.

The responses were analyzed from mid-December through early January 1981. The task force was reconvened to review the data collected, respond to their potential meaning, and offer advice regarding additional analyses that might be performed. A presentation was made to the board president to gain insights regarding how the data might be best formatted for the board's review. In addition to the survey data, archival information was presented by researchers Cooley and Bickel to the Pittsburgh Board of Education in late January 1981. These archival data represented information they had gathered about the school district in their analysis of the district's use of data for decision making. They developed a school-level file for each school that contained the following types of information: enrollment, demographic characteristics of the student population, suspensions, class size, and teacher characteristics. Student-level data included achievement test results and participation in programs such as special education and compensatory education. These data were used to amplify and supplement the findings of the needs assessment survey.

Setting the Priorities: January 1981

Cooley and Bickel met with the board and me in January 1981 to present the findings of the needs assessment. I asked the board to think about the data and identify no more than six priorities that I could begin working on with staff. Following extensive discussion, the board tentatively identified these six educational priorities for me to address:

1. Improving student achievement in the basic skills
2. Improving the quality of personnel evaluation
3. Managing enrollment decline
4. Attracting and holding students
5. Discipline
6. Low-achieving African American segregated schools

I asked the board to formally vote these priorities as the agenda for the school district at their next legislative meeting. I also asked for 6 months to work with staff members to prepare specific plans for formal adoption.

Of the six priorities, two emerged as very strong issues from all the populations sampled: improving the basic achievement skills of students and improving personnel evaluation. The message about evaluation was clear—the district had too many incompetent teachers and administrators; something had to be done about it.

Building Constituencies for the Data: February and March 1981

Following the board's approval of the priorities, Cooley and I met with each of the four groups surveyed. These meetings had two purposes: (a) to communicate the results of the survey so that all groups could review the data and ask questions about their meaning and (b) to communicate that these data were being used to formulate initiatives to address the problems. The meetings were followed by a press conference at which the survey results were presented to the general public.

The Priority Planning Process: February Through June 1981

Immediately following the vote of the board in February, I initiated a comprehensive planning process for the six priorities. The planning coordinator developed the planning process and monitored its implementation. For each of the six areas, a planning task force was identified, including union leadership, union-building representatives, highly regarded teachers and administrators, and influential community leaders. The composition of the task forces was designed to build a constituency for the initiatives. The sequence of activities used by the planning coordinator to complete the planning process is discussed in Chapter 3.

Products and Results of Priority Planning: 1981

Major program initiatives were developed for each of the six priorities established by the board. These are briefly summarized next. Several of the programs received national recognition or awards as exemplary programs.

Priority 1: Improving student achievement in the basic skills. Monitoring Achievement in Pittsburgh (MAP) was the initiative designed to improve student achievement in the basic skills. The results of the MAP math program were dramatic. In 1 year, math achievement scores increased significantly. Between 1980 and 1985, with the addition of MAP writing and reading programs, the achievement of African American students doubled and white students' increased by 50% (see Chapter 9 for a detailed presentation).

Priority 2: Improving the quality of personnel evaluation. The initiative known as Pittsburgh's Research-Based Instructional Supervisory Model (PRISM) was designed to implement this priority. PRISM focused initially on training principals to observe and confer with teachers to improve instruction and the quality of personnel evaluation. This program received several national awards. Most important, PRISM developed a spirit of professionalism among teachers and principals that paved the way for significant educational improvement in the district. The community's perception of the schools improved markedly as a result of the MAP and PRISM programs (see Chapters 9 and 10 for detailed presentations).

Priority 3: Managing enrollment decline. A comprehensive initiative for school closings was designed and implemented beginning in June 1982 and developed and approved by the board that fall. As a result, some schools were closed and schools of special emphasis, which addressed the desegregation plan and the need to improve the quality of education, were created.

Priority 4: Attracting and holding students. The major strategy for attracting students back to the public schools was aggressively marketing the district's magnet schools and a new program for gifted students. The initial plan for increasing the holding power of high schools was to focus on basic skills attainment of middle school pupils to ensure greater success in high school. Later strategies involved career magnet programs that offered employment training as a means of keeping students in school.

The emphasis on magnet programs paid huge dividends in enhancing public opinion about the quality of Pittsburgh's public education system. By the mid-1980s, parents were lining up outside magnet schools a week before sign-up day; they pitched tents and sleeping bags outside the schools to be in line for the first-come, first-served enrollments. This proved to be a public relations boon for the school district. Articles in the *Wall Street Journal,* the *Christian Science Monitor,* and local papers, along with television coverage, created the image that it was the "in thing" to have your child in a Pittsburgh Public Schools magnet program. The program became so successful that, by the late 1980s, the district had to abandon the first-come, first-served method of enrollment in favor of a lottery system. Also, the district began to develop special emphasis schools that were neighborhood schools and not magnets.

During the mid-1980s, the Pittsburgh schools were attracting close to 1,000 students per year back from private and parochial schools. By 1992, every school that had been closed in the early 1980s had to be reopened. Student enrollment was increasing so much that the district had to buy or lease closed parochial schools to accommodate them all.

A state-mandated change in the gifted program at the secondary level caused the district to change its Pittsburgh Scholars program into Centers for Advanced Study. These became so popular that large numbers of gifted students from the area's private schools were attracted back to public schools.

Priority 5: Improving the quality of discipline. A superintendent-led task force of teachers and administrators addressed consistent discipline practices. Discipline committees established in each school were to include professionals, paraprofessionals, and support staff. In-house suspension rooms were established in each school to avoid out-of-school suspensions.

A special program, The Commonwealth Classroom, was established in each middle school to train disruptive students in the socially desirable behavior necessary for integration back into the regular classroom. These initiatives created the image that the schools were safe places and were dealing effectively with disruptive pupils. The Commonwealth Classroom model was disseminated throughout Pennsylvania with support from the State Education Department.

Priority 6: Low-achieving African American segregated schools. A school improvement program (SIP) was designed and a team of professionals was assigned to six African American segregated schools or low-achieving predominantly African American schools to initiate change. The SIP team had 3 years to improve education in those schools and create a model that could be used in other schools. SIP had some remarkable successes in its first 3 years. Most of the six schools showed significant improvement; one that had ranked 57th out of 57 elementary schools in student achievement in 1980 moved into the top 20.

1986 Through 1989

The 1986 Needs Assessment Survey

The 1980 needs assessment survey had focused the attention of the board, the professional staff, and the community on the district's educational goals. These priorities were the powerful driving force for educational improvement. Gradual changes occurred in the board so that by 1986, only two members remained of the nine who voted on the 1981 priorities. Thus, I decided to readminister the same needs assessment survey and engage the new board members in assessing the district's current status.

By 1986, the district had organized and staffed its own in-house division of research and evaluation, with Paul LeMahieu as director. LeMahieu extended the survey work started by Cooley in 1980. Also by 1986, the district had disaggregated achievement data by race in addition to other data that described the state of the district.

Setting New Priorities: 1986

The board and I met with LeMahieu to review the 1986 survey and additional archival data. Following discussion of the updated data, the board asked me to pursue the initiatives implemented in 1981 and to begin planning for additional priorities clustered in the following areas:

Achievement
Fiscal responsibility
Student discipline
Prior district initiatives

The priorities for each area are listed below.

Cluster I Priorities: Achievement

- Improve the reading ability of all students with special emphasis on those who need additional help.
- Continue efforts to lower the racial achievement gap between African American and white students.
- Ensure that low-achieving students at all levels are given appropriate services to promote effective learning.
- Increase the number of students taking higher mathematics and science courses in secondary schools by increasing the quality and pacing of these courses at all levels.

Cluster II Priorities: Fiscal Responsibility

- Analyze in detail all operations to ensure that the costs of services are reasonable.
- Initiate collaboration with appropriate public and private agencies to broaden the sources of revenue for the district.
- Improve the budget development, approval, and monitoring process at all levels of policy and administration.

Cluster III Priorities: Student Discipline

- Undertake preventive measures to promote better school discipline through staff development and special programs for students.
- Promote measures to ensure consistent enforcement of the discipline code in all schools by all personnel.

Cluster IV Priorities: Sustain and Improve District Initiatives

- Sustain efforts to effectively evaluate all district personnel.
- Intensify efforts to decrease the dropout rate and sustain efforts to attract nonpublic school students to public schools.
- Support the elementary school improvement program until all schools are effective.
- Enhance efforts to involve parents and the community through volunteer programs and other initiatives.
- Sustain efforts to prepare students for entry into the workforce with the needed knowledge, skills, and attitudes.

In 1980, the board's top priority was to improve student achievement in basic skills; in 1986, achievement was still the top priority, but the goals of the board were much more specific—this was true for all of the priority areas.

In every action taken by the board between 1980 and 1986, I drew specific attention to the priority being addressed by the proposed agenda item. Thus, even with gradual changes in membership from 1980 to 1986, the board become highly conversant with the 1981 priorities and better informed about educational matters in general.

The Priority Planning Process: 1986

The planning process followed the model used in 1981. The outcomes were recommendations with proposed budgets that the board adopted in the winter of 1987. The following sections highlight a few of the programs implemented and their results. The four priorities regarding student achievement are described, as is the revenue enhancement priority for fiscal responsibility.

Cluster I Priority: Student Achievement in reading. Emphasis on reading included a continuation of the MAP program and the widespread use of the DEAR (drop everything and read) program. Selected secondary students used computer-based reading instruction. The MAP program produced gains in reading achievement, but its original atomistic approach to the teaching of reading changed to a holistic approach in the late 1980s. The DEAR program was widely implemented to improve comprehension skills and promote leisure reading. Elementary, middle, and secondary schools developed effective models for integrating DEAR into the daily schedule. The computer-based reading instruction did not meet with great success in pilot studies and was discontinued.

Cluster I Priority: Student achievement relating to the racial achievement gap. Teachers participated in staff development training that emphasized high expectations for all students, especially minority students. An observing-for-equity program was implemented as part of teacher observation, feedback, and evaluation. Steady growth was observed in the achievement of African American students from 1981 to 1987; after that time, however, efforts to close the remaining gap in achievement failed to make any further gains. A multicultural program was designed in 1989 as another means of addressing the racial achievement gap (see Chapter 9).

Cluster I Priority: Achievement for low-achieving students. Community education centers (CECs) were established in selected communities to provide elementary school students with after-school, Saturday, and summer programs in reading and math; mentoring activities were also offered. The CECs were designed to close the racial achievement gap by offering special help to minority students. Two different models of CECs were offered; one was operated by school personnel and the second by a community agency with a long record of after-school and summer programs. Both models were very effective in helping children who attended regularly.

Cluster I Priority: Student achievement in mathematics and science. For each elementary school, science specialists were identified and trained to give students hands-on science instruction. An extensive training program provided elementary teachers with the background to teach elementary school science. The district created science rooms in each elementary school to allow hands-on instruction at all grade levels.

The Pittsburgh Science Institute was developed to train and assist teachers to improve science instruction. The institute brought together a broad collection of university, business, and school personnel to have the city's best resources available to influence the quality of science education. It was recognized in a Carnegie Foundation report as the most extensive and effective locally initiated collaborative to improve science education (Atkin & Atkin, 1989).

Cluster II Priority: Revenue enhancement. A small development office established in 1983 was expanded to provide three full-time professionals who solicited financial resources from foundations, federal agencies, and individual philanthropies. From 1983 to 1992, the development office raised over $30 million from local and national private and corporate foundations and from state and federal educational agencies; this revenue supported innovative educational practices in the Pittsburgh schools.

1990 Through 1992

Setting Additional Priorities

By 1990, changes in board membership left only one person remaining from 1980. This new board became interested in the district initiatives begun in the late 1980s in response to the external evaluation audit conducted at my request (Hammond, LeMahieu, & Wallace, 1989). One recommendation offered was that the district implement a multicultural program to address the needs of African American students and reduce the racial achievement gap. The district had begun pilot testing an early childhood education program that addressed the needs of poor and minority children; the audit group suggested that it be augmented to improve student achievement. Both of these programs began formally in 1989 with the convening of communitywide task forces that developed plans and made recommendations to the board and the administration on these two important issues.

Products and Results of Priority Planning: 1990

The board reassigned the district's staff development resources to the new 1990 priorities: multicultural education and early childhood education. The early childhood program was operative in two centers that provided demonstration models for the district. With the additional resources from staff development, a 6-year phase-in plan was designed to infuse the schools with multicultural and early childhood programs.

The plan for the early childhood program called for teams made up of staff development personnel, demonstration teachers, and replacement teachers to move into a school for an extended period of time. Demonstrations of teaching techniques, formal training in new strategies, and observation and feedback sessions were provided in teachers' own classrooms. The program was housed in two elementary schools that served as development and demonstration sites.

The multicultural dissemination plan also called for on-site training of teachers in elements of this program and was initiated at the Prospect

Middle School Center for Multicultural Education. It was designed as a model that would then be disseminated to schools throughout the city. When I retired in 1992, both plans were being implemented.

The Pittsburgh Needs
Assessment Surveys in Retrospect

The needs assessment surveys put the notion of data-oriented educational leadership into operation. As a result of the surveys and subsequent data analysis, in 1980 and 1986, the board voted on specific priorities that became the agenda for the Pittsburgh schools for 10 years. These priorities brought a divided board together and rallied them to focus on achieving their agenda for the district. For an entire decade, there was virtual unanimity among the board on educational matters.

The board priorities also became the rallying point for the professionals in the district. The agenda clearly focused the attention of the professional staff on developing initiatives to address the priorities. The board's constant review and evaluation of the initiatives communicated to the staff their seriousness of purpose about educational reform.

These priorities also became the focus of fund-raising. The first appeals to private foundations in the city targeted a specific program to improve student achievement in basic skills. External funding increased rapidly with a planned program of solicitation for the Schenley High School Teacher Center, designed to improve personnel evaluation.

The priorities gave the board a means to monitor the progress of the district and to gauge where resources were being spent. Thus, my use of a data orientation to educational leadership paid significant dividends in developing a local renaissance in public education. The Pittsburgh schools gained a national and international reputation as an innovative urban district by implementing initiatives in response to priorities that emerged from data.

The Providence Story

The use of data to guide educational renewal in Providence, Rhode Island, grew out of the Public Education Fund's (PEF) initiative to rally the community to support the city's schools. The Providence Chamber of Commerce joined with the PEF to support PROBE.

The PEF had been involved in the typical activities of providing minigrants for teachers and last-dollar student scholarships and building school-business partnerships since 1985. In 1989, its director saw the potential to enable more significant change for the school district than the general PEF activities. The director convinced the Providence Teachers Union (PTU) and the school administration to endorse a community survey that would provide the basis for support of educational change. The PEF board agreed to amend the mission of the organization and take on initiatives for change in the Providence schools.

In 1991, the fund's board created the PROBE Commission independent of the PEF but under its general umbrella. At its invitation, the recently retired president of the University of Rhode Island took on the responsibility for the PROBE Commission and began working with the PEF to rally the business community on behalf of the school system.

The PROBE Survey

PROBE's first activity was a communitywide survey to (a) ascertain the current condition of the Providence schools and (b) identify specific ways to improve them. Both the school district and the union supported the survey. The president of the PTU viewed the survey as a way of communicating to the general public the quality that she believed existed in the Providence schools. The superintendent of schools saw that the survey was consistent with a strategic planning initiative that he was about to begin.

The PROBE Commission began its work as an external catalyst for the support and improvement of the Providence Public Schools. With financial support from the Providence Chamber of Commerce and the business community, the PROBE staff was assembled and began its work. The PROBE staff took seriously the need to gather data to substantiate its description of the status quo of the Providence schools. The staff was determined to (a) listen carefully to citizens, parents, teachers, and administrators about their perceptions of the state of the school district and (b) make recommendations for improvements based on data from stakeholders and other relevant historical and comparative data.

The PROBE Commission was composed of 33 community members; approximately half of whom had children in the public schools. About half of the members also represented minority groups present in the city. The commission was organized into six study committees; they dealt with (a) governance, (b) budget and facilities, (c) teachers and curriculum, (d) students, (e) parents, and (f) community. All the committees recruited additional members to help accomplish their tasks.

The PROBE staff used three major sources for the study: survey data, archival data, and comparative data. Survey information was collected from questionnaires mailed to each population group represented in the study committee areas. Existing data from the Providence Public School archives were collected and analyzed. Comparative data were gathered from 11 other cities in the northeastern United States that were judged to be comparable to Providence; these were used to illustrate similarities and differences between Providence schools and comparison schools.

The methods used to develop survey instruments for each stakeholder group followed this pattern: The PROBE staff conducted individual interviews with representatives of each population to be surveyed and also held focus group discussions. The language of the stakeholders was used to describe the conditions in the schools; the staff did not want to use a generic survey instrument that would have limited relevance to Providence.

The PROBE Survey Findings

Data were collected and analyzed during an 18-month period and produced findings that focused on 10 issues; 39 specific PROBE recommendations were organized around these issues. A brief description of the salient findings related to each of the 10 issues follows.

1. *Communication and interpersonal relations.* This issue was common to virtually every group interviewed. Whether referring to teachers, principals, or students, there appeared to be a "we versus they" problem. Different groups believed that their superiors didn't listen to what they had to say. Parents were the only group that indicated that they were pleased that teachers listened to them.

2. *Diversity.* During the 1980s, the student population increased about 20%; the number of Hispanic students more than doubled, the Asian student population increased by one third, the number of African American students remained the same, and the white population declined significantly. More than 68 different languages and dialects are spoken in the homes of Providence schoolchildren.

3. *Passive and active learning.* Students communicated a strong need to be more actively involved in learning. They complained about the amount of time they had to listen to teachers talk. Teachers also expressed an interest in wanting to engage students more actively in learning activities.

4. *Differences between elementary and secondary schools.* All the indicators describing elementary schools were positive. Virtually all the indicators

about middle and secondary schools were less so; students in these schools believed that they were not sufficiently challenged or treated with dignity.

5. *Differences in students' perceptions of the high schools.* Two of the five high schools in Providence were regarded very positively by students; one of these was an alternative school. Students indicated that in these schools, teachers maintain their interest in the subjects, present topics of interest, and provide opportunities to work on projects with other students; students were less positive on all of these attributes for the other schools.

6. *Equality of opportunity for students.* The data indicated that the nonwhite student populations were seriously underrepresented in the district's rigorous academic programs. Furthermore, the limited English proficiency program and special education programs were judged as having severe problems by the Rhode Island Department of Education and the U.S. Department of Education; continued funding of these two programs had been threatened. The findings indicated a serious need to address the issue of equity.

7. *Professional development.* The district spent less than one tenth of 1% of its budget on staff development. Those professional development activities offered to teachers and administrators were judged to be inadequate. School board members did not participate in any board development activities.

8. *Evaluation and accountability.* The data indicated that professional evaluation was generally inconsistent or seriously lacking. Teachers and administrators believed that incompetence in teaching and administration was not being addressed and that excellence in performance was not recognized or rewarded.

9. *Revenue and expenditures.* Survey data of other districts indicated that Providence spent considerably fewer dollars per pupil than most cities of comparable size, averaging almost $1,000 less per pupil. Much of the disparity came from a lack of state funding for urban education compared with other states.

10. *Data and self-knowledge.* The survey indicated that the school district has an inadequate system to provide sufficient information for effective analysis of the district's strengths and weaknesses.

The 10 key issues and the 39 recommendations presented in the PROBE report identified conditions that could and should be improved. In the core of the issues were the seeds for solutions. Furthermore, the data suggested that the key stakeholders were willing to work to improve education for students and the quality of work life for professionals. Thus this information, along with programs developed by the administration, set the stage for a renewal of the Providence schools.

PROBE Recommendations

The PROBE report went far beyond the presentation of data by proposing the 39 recommendations for the improvement of conditions, operations, and programs. These recommendations were grouped in three categories—people, structures, and resources—and were presented in the following framework: "Imagine what you will see in the Providence Schools when people change, when structures change, and when resources change." The PROBE Commission also recommended a time line for the implementation of the recommendations.

Of the 39 specific recommendations presented in the PROBE report published by the PEF (1993), 10 are extracted here (with original numbering) as illustrations:

"When Structures Change"
   2. Create smaller learning environments.
   3. Lengthen the student working day.
   6. Lengthen teacher working year.
   7. Redesign the process for school board appointments.
   20. Establish goals by and within each school.
   21. Establish site management at five prototype schools.

"When Resources Change"
   22. Institute professional development and evaluation of the school board.
   24. Institute professional development and evaluation of principals.
   25. Institute professional development and evaluation of teachers: mentoring, peer coaching, intervention, recognition of excellence.
   33. Increase business community involvement in schools. (pp. 29-100)

The PROBE Commission

The unique aspect of the PROBE Commission report is that it represents a stakeholder's assessment of the problems and prospects of the community's schools. The PEF created a permanent structure, the PROBE Council, to oversee the implementation of the recommendations and gather funding to enable change. The PROBE Council has become the action arm of the PEF to promote lasting reform. That an organization external to the schools has taken the position to rally broad community support for the Providence schools in a direct, interventionist manner is remarkable; that it uses a data orientation to identify needs and opportunities is exemplary. The fact that the organization has continued to support the change initiative from the outside may be worthy of emulation by other cities.

The president of the PEF expressed the continuing interest of the community as follows (PEF, 1993):

> The PROBE Council has accepted the challenge to act as facilita-tor and catalyst to ensure that all parties from the Mayor, City Council, the School Board, the School Department, the Teachers Union, business leaders, and others move toward change.
>
> The role of the PROBE Council, as PEF envisions it, is to require accountability so that reform efforts will become a reality. To that end, PEF will develop and issue an annual report card documenting progress toward the implementation of all PROBE recommendations. (p. 106)

Progress in Providence

Following the analyses of the surveys and the preparation of the draft report, the PROBE staff briefed each stakeholder group on the findings. The PROBE Commission wanted to be sure that each of the groups was fully informed prior to the broad dissemination of the report. It was of great importance that the school board, the school administration, and the teach-ers union be fully aware because the recommendations dealt directly with all of them. The briefings were important because the media tend to sensationalize such findings and do not always present a complete story.

After the release of the report in January 1993, the school board voted five priorities for the administration to address immediately. These priori-ties delineated an exceptional long-term plan based on data; significant progress has been made already in several of the priority areas. The mayor agreed to initiate a new process for the appointment of school board members by selecting them from a list provided by a blue-ribbon committee.

The administration and the teachers union also endorsed the PROBE report. In 1991, the administration embarked on the development of a strategic plan to improve the quality of education in the school district. This work began under the former superintendent and has continued under the current superintendent. The PROBE recommendations address issues that the district's administration has been working on for 3 years.

I had the opportunity to review the work of the school district in August 1994. The Providence schools have made substantial progress in addressing some of the PROBE recommendations as well as their own agenda. Very significant advances have been made in the areas of special education and bilingual education. New directors have been appointed for each program, all of the compliance issues for special education have been addressed, and a very sophisticated program for bilingual education is being implemented with the collaboration of the diverse multilingual community.

The comprehensive nature of planning by the district is impressive. The implementation of the plans, however, is just beginning. The ultimate success of the Providence school district in reaching its own goals and those included in the PROBE report depends on the development of an effective working relationship with the PTU and the willingness of the union to move on some significant issues. Some of the most important issues relate to teacher evaluation, site-based management, and a hiring process that does not give preference to substitute teachers. Movement by the union on these and other issues is needed to bring about the structural changes necessary to achieve substantial reform.

The Future of PROBE

The PROBE Commission is still brokering relationships between the school district and the community. During the summer of 1994, PROBE received substantial funding to support teacher training for the creation of smaller learning units in secondary schools. The commission continues to be the voice of the community in urging and supporting change in the Providence schools. The ultimate success of the commission depends on the extent to which progress is made in the school district.

The business community in Providence may not fully understand the complexity of change in educational institutions. The tendency of many groups is toward "quick fixes" and impatience with planning and implementation. The reality, however, is that it will take the school district from 3 to 5 years to demonstrate substantial results; the district will have to find ways of communicating its progress and provide evidence that things are changing if they are to sustain community support. Will the city of Providence be willing to wait 3 to 5 years? The PROBE Commission can help inform the public of the time it takes to institute substantial change.

The district's administration has prepared a report card to help convey progress; it should complement the PROBE report card and help sustain the movement toward educational improvement.

SUMMARY

The use of data to guide educational leadership and renewal in the cities of Pittsburgh and Providence has been described. Although the initiators differed in the two cities, the conditions that gave rise to the need to define problems and pose solutions were similar. Both Pittsburgh and Providence had school districts that, in the eyes of the stakeholders, needed significant educational change.

Data analyses drove educational planning and reform in Pittsburgh. A 1980 needs assessment survey set the stage for educational reform in the first half of the decade; the 1986 survey prompted additional educational priorities for the second half of the decade. It was the Pittsburgh school district and board that made judgments of success, which were confirmed to the public through a public relations campaign.

The PROBE survey has set the conditions for educational improvement in Providence. Since the PROBE recommendations came from a public agency, the agenda is a public one. Thus, to a large extent, the public will make the judgment regarding its success.

There is potential for significant reform in Providence. Sustaining the effort will require continued public support through the PROBE Commission, data collection to confirm progress in the school district, and active collaboration of the teachers union. Providence presents the interesting story of a Public Education Fund facilitating significant change in an urban school district.

9

Improving Student Achievement Through Monitoring, Alternative Methods of Assessment, and Special Programs

Parents and the general public most often judge the quality of education on students' performance on standardized tests of academic achievement. Thus, to improve the quality of education in the eyes of these constituents, achievement scores need to improve. High schools are also typically judged on the basis of average scores on the SAT. Both types of tests are woefully inadequate to judge the quality of education in any school district.

Standardized achievement tests assess very low-level skills and tend to trivialize education. Yet the test publishing houses have been unwilling to take the risk of developing new forms of assessing student learning, apparently too concerned about maintaining and improving the bottom line for their stockholders to venture from the traditional tests. Parents and the general public think they know what standardized test scores mean; they believe that high scores mean that students are getting a good education. Colleges and universities use SAT scores as a major criterion for admission.

School districts are caught in a bind. Standardized achievement tests are the "coin of the realm" and school districts have to live with them. Yet many educators believe that authentic measures offer much better assessment of student learning and communication of educational achievement to parents and the general public.

The current movement toward more authentic measures of student achievement focuses on portfolio assessment, exhibitions, and profiles (Archbald & Newmann, 1988). Portfolio assessment in student writing is beginning to have a national effect. It judges student writing against agreed-on standards; this is far more accurate for evaluating writing achievement than multiple choice items on a standardized test. Exhibitions of student work, as in the tradition of science fairs, are an effective means of judging student work. Profiles of student accomplishment over a period of time also provide a valuable chronology of student work.

Most school districts interested in authentic assessment deal with the dilemma of how to also improve results on standardized tests. Superintendents have to work with professionals and parents to pave the way for more authentic forms of assessing, recording, and reporting student learning. This chapter presents a model of student monitoring designed to improve achievement scores on standardized tests and two models that exemplify the movement toward authentic student assessment in Pittsburgh. Descriptions are also given about special achievement programs in Pittsburgh and other school districts.

Improving Student Achievement in the Basic Skills

A program called Monitoring Achievement in Pittsburgh (MAP) was designed to improve student performance in basic skills attainment. It grew out of my experience in implementing a system of skills achievement monitoring (SAM) when I was a superintendent in Fitchburg, Massachusetts. SAM was validated for statewide dissemination in the 1970s by the Massachusetts Department of Education.

MAP Assumptions

MAP became a comprehensive program to improve student achievement. It was named as one of the ten best educational programs in American education during the decade of the 1980s (Lewis, 1988). The program was based on the following assumptions:

1. Classroom teachers are an untapped resource for educational improvement.
2. Principals must be instructional leaders.
3. Teachers must have support to innovate.
4. Multiple imperfect measures need to be used to effectively assess student achievement.

Many of the educational innovations of the 1960s tried to create teacher-proof curricula and instructional strategies that teachers couldn't "mess up," which communicated a lack of respect for teachers (Wallace & Reidy, 1980). Assumption 1 indicated that teachers needed to be respected and tapped as a primary resource for creating solutions designed to increase student achievement. MAP programs were designed for teachers by teachers; teacher liaisons in each building provided on-the-spot assistance for others who needed help in implementing the program. Teachers wrote the objectives, created test items, identified instructional materials, and designed staff development programs.

Assumption 2 asserted that principals must be instructional leaders, which grew out the effective schools research movement (Edmonds, 1979) and held that principals set the tone for educational achievement in their buildings. They could exercise effective instructional leadership by setting high expectations for students and faculty and by monitoring closely the achievement of students. Close monitoring of student progress is the hallmark of the principal who functions as an instructional leader.

Assumption 3 stated that teachers needed support from central administration and from building principals to implement effectively new educational programs. Professional development training, coaching, and feedback are necessary for teachers to implement successfully any new program, and they need to be involved in designing the support interventions.

Assumption 4 addressed the concept of multiple imperfect measures. Any measure of student achievement is imperfect. The imperfections may emerge from the lack of comprehensiveness of the instruments themselves, the modes of administration, the interpretation, or technical deficiencies in the items. Making definitive judgments about student performance on the basis of a single instrument is risky. Thus, the concept of multiple measures advises teachers and administrators not to place undue reliance on any single assessment of student achievement; rather, accuracy is enhanced to the degree that multiple measures of student performance are combined to make judgments.

MAP Components

In addition to the assumptions listed, the program had five components: (a) skill expectations, (b) focused instruction, (c) focused monitoring, (d) instructional materials, and (e) staff development.

Skill Expectations

Skill expectation was the cornerstone of MAP. Teachers identified the most important learning outcomes for each subject at each grade level. (Approximately 20 of the most important outcomes in third-grade reading were specified, for example.) The expectations selected were those that would best guarantee that students could be successful at that grade level and were chosen independent of any reference to standardized tests; they represented teachers' judgment about what they deemed most important for students to know and be able to do. Communicating these expectations to students, parents, and administrators established an explicit framework of skill acquisition.

Focused Instruction

Focused instruction required teachers to devote time in a given skill subject on MAP learning outcomes. The rule of thumb was that 60% of instructional time should be allocated to MAP outcomes to ensure that virtually every student developed competence in the basic skills.

Focused Monitoring

Focused monitoring provided for tests to be given every 6 to 9 weeks depending on the subject. Tests included one item per objective, and students were tested on all objectives on every test even though they might not have had instruction on all items. All items were designed to create anticipation in students regarding what they were expected to learn in a given year.

Teachers received a computer printout of an analysis-of-errors matrix identifying each student's performance on each objective. By analyzing these data, teachers could group or regroup students for instruction. Obviously, testing for one item per objective required teachers to use other measures to judge student mastery; they relied on homework, class work, and other sources of evidence to group students for instruction. Students were given a computer printout to take home to their parents with results of their performance on each objective and a list of items for which instruction had been provided.

Instructional Materials

Instructional materials and staff development provided teachers with the necessary support to implement the MAP program. Teachers chose the instructional materials to supplement regular textbooks that they believed promoted student competence.

Staff Development

Teachers involved in the development of the various components were convened to design a staff development program for their peers. These teachers were also directly involved in the implementation of the training.

Development of the MAP Program

Groups of teachers were selected to develop each component using the assumptions to guide their work. Selected teachers who were highly respected by their peers were convened for each subject and each grade level.

The groups that developed the skill expectations identified approximately 20 of the most important skills for students to master at their grade level; they found this to be a difficult task. On the basis of my previous experience with achievement monitoring, I knew that teachers could handle approximately 20 outcomes effectively and without difficulty. Selecting about 20 learning outcomes for a grade level for a year required teachers to think carefully about what skills were most important and what enabling skills were required in order for students to be successful.

Once the groups completed this task, the skill expectations were sent out to all teachers of that specific subject and grade for review and comment. Thus, the entire teaching staff had an opportunity to participate and comment on what they believed to be important for students. The skill expectations were also evaluated against criteria established by national organizations in each field to ensure content validity (e.g., National Council of Teachers of Mathematics).

Once the expectations were developed and reviewed, a second group of teachers developed test items for each objective. This task was one for which teachers initially felt unqualified; however, experience demonstrated that they were able to develop good items. When sufficient items were developed to prepare several forms of the MAP tests, selected ones were sent out to all teachers for review. Each teacher had the opportunity to comment on test items.

The Testing and Evaluation Office worked with the Computer Services Division to develop and pilot test the computer forms that were provided to teachers, students, and parents. The curriculum, testing, and computer departments handled the logistics of distributing, collecting, and scoring of tests.

A third group of teachers was then convened to recommend instructional materials needed to focus instruction on the outcomes. Teachers reviewed existing texts and supporting materials and made recommendations for additional materials, if needed.

When expectations, tests, and instructional materials were identified, selected teachers from each group were asked to help design the staff development needed to implement the program in each school. Part of the plan for staff development was to identify one teacher in each school who could be a resource person for others who needed additional help and who provided assistance to the principal in the program implementation.

Another important part of MAP was a parent training program. Parents needed training to interpret the test results and review the annual set of expectations for their children.

Specific MAP Programs

MAP began with a math program in 1981, and programs in writing, reading, and critical thinking followed; in the mid-1980s, programs in social studies and science were added. MAP programs gained such high status in the district in the early 1980s that other subject matter supervisors wanted a MAP monitoring system so that they could have equal billing with math, reading, and writing.

MAP Math. Mathematics is the easiest subject with which to begin such a system. Generally, it is easy for teachers to reach agreement on math learning outcomes.

MAP Reading. Reading is one of the most difficult areas for which to develop a monitoring system because of the students' needs to acquire many discrete skills; it was difficult for teachers to come to consensus on a limited number of reading outcomes. In addition, there remained a controversy between phonetic and sight approaches to the teaching of reading.

MAP Writing. Writing comprises a relatively easy set of skills to monitor. The major choice in this area is whether to use analytic or holistic scoring. Training teachers to teach writing, however, is a formidable task. Most teachers of English in middle and secondary schools have had little training in teaching writing. Elementary teachers usually have had no training. A district will have to invest a significant amount of time and dollars to train teachers to first become writers themselves and then to teach them to teach writing to students. On the other hand, training teachers to score student papers reliably can be accomplished in a few hours.

MAP Critical Thinking. The MAP critical thinking program communicated to teachers and parents that teaching this skill was an important goal for the school district. It was intended to express the value that competence in basic skills is not enough. The critical thinking program took a writing approach to achieve its goals. Staff development programs focused on training teachers to ask higher-order questions as a part of their regular instructional routine; they were trained to rate students' writing analytically to judge attainment of critical thinking skills.

Several different programs employed to promote higher-order questioning in the district's classrooms used different terminology. In 1985, to avoid confusion and gain consensus among curriculum specialists and teachers, the district developed its own Pittsburgh's Categories of Questioning; these were synthesized from several approaches used nationally to promote critical thinking. A document-based essay approach was used to judge the students' ability to think critically. They were typically given different accounts of a historical event, for example, and asked to compare and contrast the texts (documents) and take a position based on evidence. The program provided model lessons for teachers to use. The critical thinking program turned out to be somewhat duplicative of the writing assessment program and was ultimately replaced by it.

Results of the MAP Program

The MAP program provided an instructional focus for the school district. Although the careful monitoring of student achievement made some teachers uncomfortable, the program did have an effect on teachers, students, and parents. Student achievement in the basic skills rose dramatically: Math and writing scores were quick to move; reading took a little longer to show a significant increase.

In 1984, the district disaggregated scores by race for the first time. The results indicated that African American students performed less well than their white student counterparts. The data demonstrated that, although the achievement of African American students had doubled from the early 1980s to 1986, it was still significantly below that of white students because their scores had also improved. By 1986, more than 50% of the African American students scored at or above national norms; more than 80% of the white students scored above national norms. But the racial achievement gap was not closing; to this date, the gap still remains.

By the late 1980s, the focus in mathematics turned from an emphasis on computation to one on developing mathematical concepts and problem solving; in reading, attention turned from mastery of discrete skills to an emphasis on comprehension and reading for enjoyment. By that time, the district was also moving forward on its secondary school examination program to promote higher expectations and higher achievement in all subject areas. In 1993, the board decided that the MAP program had served its purpose and discontinued it.

Improving Student
Achievement Through Examinations

The Syllabus Examination Program

The MAP program just described was designed to improve the basic skills achievement of the district in direct response to the board's 1981 priority (see Chapter 8). Basic skills, however, are not the end goal of education; they are the enabling skills that allow a student to become educated. An emphasis on basic skills achievement without a commitment to teach the application of those skills to higher educational purposes is shortsighted.

The European examination system has been a time-honored tradition to prepare students for higher education. Although this system has some serious disadvantages, it does create high expectations for students (Wallace, 1985a). Pittsburgh initiated a syllabus examination program (SEP) to begin to establish high expectations of achievement for secondary school students.

While MAP was in development, I met with the curriculum directors and the evaluation specialists to sketch out an examination system. In addition to raising expectations, the system was to also stimulate changes in instructional practices in the district's secondary classrooms. A paper that I presented at an Educational Testing Service Conference outlined the purposes of that program (Wallace, 1985a).

SEP was modeled after traditional European examinations; it was to include a comprehensive syllabus, explicit learning outcomes, and sample questions with acceptable written responses. There was, however, an important difference. One disadvantage of European systems is that the student has only one opportunity to demonstrate competence; thus, great emphasis is placed on his or her performance, and the experience can produce high student anxiety. Significant decisions are made about the academic or vocational future of a student on the basis of his or her performance on one examination. SEP was designed to have some characteristics of European exams, but the pressure to perform on a single exam was removed.

SEP exams were to be administered quarterly in each subject during the school year; the purpose of giving them quarterly was to provide students and teachers with the ability to gauge student progress toward the course goals. In social studies, for example, a 10th-grade course on world cultures had four examinations; the exams were not to be used as the sole criteria to determine students' grades. Using the concept of multiple imperfect measures, the grades on quarterly examinations could be used along with other data gathered by teachers to judge student progress. The final exam, for instance, could be a significant factor in determining a student's final grade.

The SEP program used extensively the concept of document-based questions; these are often included in advanced placement examinations, which have been part of American secondary education for many years. Document-based questions typically provide students with two differing perspectives of an event. They are asked to analyze the documents and, in an essay response, take a position and defend it with evidence from the documents along with other information they wish to introduce.

The document-based portion of the SEP exams was very similar to the MAP critical thinking essays. Secondary students had begun writing critical thinking essays in the primary grades; this type of writing continued in the upper elementary and middle schools. Thus, secondary students had prior experience in these types of writing tasks before the SEP examination program.

The SEP program was built on the expectation that classroom discourse in secondary schools would promote analytic thinking. The Pittsburgh categories of questioning, described earlier, provided a framework for classroom discussion that would encourage critical thinking. Thus, there was a widespread emphasis throughout the grades on thinking and writing skills that would enable students to perform well on the SEP exams.

Effects of the Syllabus Examination and MAP Program on Teachers

Curriculum specialists responsible for developing and implementing the MAP and SEP programs were asked to reflect on their 12 years of experience in promoting student learning in the Pittsburgh Schools (G. Morris, D. Briars, & J. Eresh, personal communication, December 5, 1994). Here are some of their comments:

> The MAP and SEP programs provided a unified effort to improve the quality of education in the Pittsburgh schools; they clearly focused the attention of the district's teachers and administrators on instruction.

> MAP and SEP brought the teachers in the district together and provided a sense of a K through 12 continuum of learning outcomes for students.

> MAP and SEP provided teachers with very clear expectations for themselves and students; MAP and SEP fostered a sense of accountability and paved the way for outcome-based education.

> The SEP math curricula in secondary schools helped to bring about significant changes in the teaching of mathematics.

> The formation of SEP programs offered a significant professional growth experience for those teachers who engaged in curriculum development work.

> SEP joined curriculum, instruction, and assessment in the minds and in the practice of secondary teachers; SEP exams and curricula are still being used in the district.

The MAP program in reading focused too much on discrete objectives and not enough on important outcomes such as the enjoyment of reading.

MAP objectives tended to be used by elementary and middle school teachers primarily to improve student scores on standardized tests.

MAP tended to take a linear view of learning; in some subject matters that is not appropriate.

Improving Student Achievement
Through Alternative Assessment

As discussed in Chapter 4, the essence of authentic assessment is that students are expected to demonstrate knowledge or skills that directly represent the learning tasks in which they were engaged. The use of portfolios is gaining widespread use in American education, including collections of work in progress so that students can, in part, assess their own growth in learning. The sections that follow describe the development in Pittsburgh of a portfolio culture in the classrooms.

Arts PROPEL

In 1991, the Arts PROPEL program was named one of the world's ten best (Chideya, 1991). It began in 1986 as a joint venture of the Pittsburgh Public Schools, Harvard University's Project Zero, and Educational Testing Service; the Rockefeller Foundation brought these three institutions together to explore different ways of assessing student achievement. The project was built on Howard Gardner's (1983) concept of multiple intelligences; it was designed to develop instructional and assessment techniques that would allow students to demonstrate their intelligence in ways other than IQ tests.

PROPEL was built around the three concepts of production, reflection, and perception. *Production* refers to the creation of a piece of work that is central to the subject being studied. The student is expected to generate a product that demonstrates fundamental concepts in a specific domain. *Reflection* refers to the thinking that a student performs as he or she engages in the process of producing a work. The student is expected to be analytical about the processes used and be able to critique the work. PROPEL is designed to foster reflectiveness in the students about their own work and that of their peers. *Perception* refers to the ability of students to be fully aware of their environment in general and, specifically, to be aware of the conditions that surround the development of a product. Through production, reflection, and perception, students are encouraged to develop their sensory awareness of the environment as they create products that reflect their emerging knowledge and intelligence.

Assessment in PROPEL

PROPEL views assessment as a natural part of the instructional process, a learning episode rather than the mere transmission of a grade. Students learn to assess their own work and the work of their peers and engage with teachers in the assessment of their progress toward the completion of a piece of work. Considerable emphasis is placed on developing instructional techniques and learning experiences that incorporate production, reflection, and perception. The fields of art, music, and creative writing were the foci for a 5-year program to develop and implement the PROPEL approach to teaching and assessment.

Domain Projects in PROPEL

The teacher's role in PROPEL is to be a mentor-coach for students rather than the dispenser of knowledge. Instruction is organized into domain projects that extend over a period of several weeks and (a) address central issues and concepts in a subject (art, music, or writing); (b) integrate opportunities for production, reflection, and perception; and (c) use assessment as part of the learning process. The projects are used to

deepen the student's understanding of the subject of study;

emphasize process as well as product;

provide opportunities for self-assessment, peer assessment, and teacher-student assessment; and

incorporate assessment to revise work in progress.

Projects may include a work of visual art, a musical composition, an ensemble performance, a poem, or a play.

Journals and Portfolios in PROPEL

Central to the learning process in PROPEL is the use of journals and portfolios, and teachers create this culture in their classrooms. Portfolios are used to monitor the developmental learning of students—they are not used exclusively as collections of students' best works. Teachers and students use them to track the development of domain projects and to guide the students in the assessment of their work. The portfolio assessment process is central to the development of reflective powers and habits.

Journals are another important component of PROPEL, and they provide another means for reflection and self-assessment. Students are encouraged to record their activities and their reaction to experiences. Journals can take many forms, such as diaries or double-entry notebooks. In a double-entry notebook, students can record their experiences in one column and their reactions in the other. Teachers review the journals regularly and write comments to the students in the journal. Thus, the journal becomes another communication device between teacher and student.

Implementing PROPEL

A team effort is required to implement PROPEL. Teachers and supervisors need an orientation to the PROPEL philosophy and the use of domain projects. They need to work together to experience the potential of domain projects and the assessment process; then they should share their reflections on their experience. If possible, they should observe an experienced PROPEL teacher in action. As teachers gain experience, they can add more domain projects and continue to share with one another about their experiences.

Skilled PROPEL teachers claim that the focus on production, reflection, and perception has significantly changed the way they structure the curriculum and teach students. One of the most significant changes relates to the way teachers look at student growth rather than merely judging a product. The development of reflective attitudes in students and a climate of reflectiveness in the classroom is one of the hallmarks of PROPEL.[1]

Improving Student Achievement
Through Special Programs

Pupil assessment and monitoring, in my judgment, is one of the most significant ways to improve student performance. My stance is based on a one-to-one correspondence between what is assessed or monitored and the content and methods of instruction. Certain student needs can be addressed only through special program content and methods, such as programs for exceptional children, multicultural educational programs, and vocational programs. The following sections will review the Pittsburgh multicultural program and selected vocational programs.

Multicultural Education

Many of the African American educators with whom I worked support the notion that special programs are needed to improve the quality of education for African American students. Through such programs, students gain a positive image of themselves, their cultures, and the cultures of other ethnic or racial groups. The basic assumption is that to learn effectively, minority students need to have a positive image of themselves as learners. Developing such an image requires, in the minds of these educators, that students know and respect their own culture.

The multicultural program in Pittsburgh grew out of a perceived need to address these issues. An independent program audit conducted for the schools in 1988 included a recommendation that the district design and implement a multicultural program to improve educational achievement for the 52% of the district's students who were African American (Hammond, LeMahieu, & Wallace, 1989). The main focus of multicultural programs is expressed by researchers Nettles, McHugh, and Gottfredson (1994) at Johns Hopkins University as follows:

> A key aspect for multicultural education is that it will help build pride in group identity, commitment to education and a sense of community among Black and Latino students. By doing so, it may weaken one of the impediments to more educational success among those groups who now fare worst in school and in the economy. One key to achieving this aspiration is making the context and the mode of instruction responsive to diversity in learning styles. (p. 8)

With support from the board of education and local and national foundations, the Pittsburgh schools launched a multicultural education program in 1989 designed around five geopolitical cultures (Bennett, 1990). The instructional component of the program focused on infusing substantive multicultural content about these cultures into relevant curricula. Another objective was to train students in conflict resolution as a means of dealing with issues that arise from differing cultural perceptions. A major focus of the Pittsburgh program was to train teachers to identify the learning styles of pupils and adjust teaching styles to achieve student commitment to learning (see Chapter 10). The program design drew on the highly regarded multicultural program in Portland, Oregon.

The Career Academies

Another important way of improving student achievement is through programs that (a) capture their interest, (b) engage them actively in authentic learning, and (c) keep them coming to school through graduation. The work of Firestone and his colleagues clearly identifies perceived relevance of schoolwork to work outside of school as a key variable in students' continuing participation in schoolwork (Firestone, Rosenblum, & Webb, 1987).

The Business and Finance Academy. Fully described in Chapter 11, this is an academic program specifically designed to link the academic studies of students to the banking industry.

The Public Safety Academy. This program was designed and implemented to prepare high school students in Pittsburgh to pursue careers, following graduation, with the police force, fire department, or paramedic rescue teams. Developed in collaboration with the Department of Public Safety, it offered students the academic background and the skills required for these departments. A positive aspect of the program was assisting the city in meeting its affirmative action goals by identifying and preparing African American and female students, among others, for positions in public safety. Orientation and work experiences while in school and summer employment prepared students for these careers; they observed firsthand and participated in the operations of the police and fire academies.

Promoting Student Achievement Through
Special Programs in Rural Communities

Two rural communities used special programs to improve student interest and achievement. At Presque Isle High School in Maine, test data and pressure from students were used to stimulate the development of a new program to improve writing skills. In Ten Sleep, Wyoming, a technology program to connect that small mountain community to the outside world was developed as a means of enriching student achievement.

Presque Isle, Maine:
Using Computers to Improve Writing

Located near the Canadian border, Presque Isle High School houses 700 students and is part of a school district that serves five other communities. Presque Isle, with 10,000 residents, is the largest; the other five communities have a combined population of 5,000 residents.

The Presque Isle schools maintain their per pupil expenditure at about $500 less than Maine's state average for high schools. Even with limited resources, the high school produces impressive results through technology (R. Durost, personal communication, March 7, 1995). Presque Isle High School was recognized as a National School of Excellence by the United States Department of Education in 1991 and the America's Best Schools program named it the top high school in Maine in 1993. One of the major reasons for the awards is the way in which the high school uses computers to improve students' writing ability.

Computerization at the high school began in 1983 when the school administration and faculty updated the business department and explored using computers in math and science. College preparatory students noticed that their friends who took word processing in the business department got their research papers and other schoolwork completed in much less time; the college prep students pressured the administration to make computers available to them for writing term papers.

In 1985, the test results in writing for students in Presque Isle High concerned the faculty and administration; on average, their students scored 20 points below the state mean on the Maine Educational Assessment (MEA) in writing. The faculty and administration decided on a two-pronged approach to improve student writing ability. First, they took a process-writing approach, which involved extensive consultations with students, revisions after the initial draft, and one-on-one review of written products. Second, the faculty decided that the best way to encourage students to write was to give them the opportunity to use word processing software, making the drafting and revising of text more palatable.

The high school now has 200 computers in five computer laboratories throughout the school. The largest lab houses 50 computers and the four others each have between 20 and 40. The faculty and the administration take the position that every student should have a computer to work on because sharing a computer results in unproductive use of time. The laboratory approach is proving superior to having a few computers in each classroom, although some teachers have computers in their classrooms for use as teaching tools. Each of the computer laboratories has 80% to 100% use for each period of the school day.

Although the business department was the catalyst for the use of computers, the English department is the heaviest user of computer laboratories. Students in English classes spend one day per week in the laboratories improving their writing skills and creating written products.

The use of computers has made a significant improvement in students' writing ability. The 1994 graduating seniors had raised their writing scores by 100 points on the MEA from the time they were tested in the 8th grade to the time they were tested as high school juniors, going from 20 points below the Maine average to 80 points above the mean. (The scores on the MEA range from 100 to 400; the MEA is administered to Grades 4, 8, and 11.)

Attached to Presque Isle High School is the Regional Vocational Technology Center, used by Presque Isle High juniors and seniors and students from the five other schools in the region. They spend one half day per week at the technology center; computers are used extensively in drafting, graphic arts, and natural resources programs.

The computer technology coordinator works with faculty members to promote the use of computers in all subjects. If one or two teachers show an interest in using specific software in their classes, he works with them.

The coordinator provides teachers with as much assistance and support as needed to be successful. These teachers then become role models and advocates for their peers. The approach facilitates the use of computers as tools for learning, teaching, and working for students, teachers, and administrators. The coordinator ensures that the hardware and software are easy to use. There are no mandates from the administration for computer use. The coordinator's ability to work with teachers in a nonthreatening, supportive manner is key to the widespread use of computers.

To make the use of computers in high school productive for students, the teaching of keyboarding skills now takes place in the middle schools. The middle schools employ computer technology aides to oversee the keyboard training of middle school students; both direct instruction and computer software are used. Instruction in keyboarding is still offered in the high school for students who move into the district or for those students who need additional skill development.

The fact that the Presque Isle district operates on limited financial resources makes the computerization of the high school even more impressive. The administration made a conscious decision to invest in computers to provide the students with a tool that will help them in advanced schooling and in the work world. The administration has made computer technology a major priority for instruction through a very thoughtful approach; they are willing to give up other things to maintain the level of technology within the dollars available per pupil.

Ten Sleep, Wyoming:
Technology Instruction to Improve Curriculum

Ten Sleep is a rural community of 300 residents located in the Big Horn Mountain basin (L. Anderson, personal communication, February 24, 1995). The 157 students in K through 12 are housed in one school building and travel as far as 40 miles; the nearest community is 27 miles away, and the nearest large community is 4 hours away.

Ten Sleep High School offers a comprehensive program that includes college prep courses, such as physics, chemistry, and calculus. Foreign language classes in Spanish, German, and French are available through satellite programming from San Antonio, Texas.

The Ten Sleep School District offers an exceptionally innovative program in technology education that began in 1990. The principal and the industrial arts teacher submitted a successful grant proposal to the State of Wyoming; the funding allowed the school to convert a conventional industrial arts classroom into a technology lab.

The lab was organized to incorporate computers and video technology. The district used the Technology Lab 2000 program from Creative Learning Systems, Inc. to initiate its program, but it has since developed its own program to meet the needs of the students.

Technology for Elementary Students

Following the implementation of the high school program, the technology teacher worked with elementary teachers, parents, the board of education, and members of the community over a 2-year period to design an elementary technology program.

The program is incorporated into various curriculum areas rather than being taught independently. Students learn to use the keyboard and computers not as isolated skills but rather to promote learning in math, science, art, English, and so forth. One aim of the program is to enable students to understand that technology is here to stay and is integrated with their life and career aspirations.

Pupils in kindergarten and first grade start to learn about technology by using Lego building blocks. As pupils advance through the primary grades, they add motors and fans to the products that they make. In the middle grades, they use bigger motors and motorized Legos to make models. In 1994, the students in the middle grades used the computer to draft a model of a flight simulator.

Technology at the High School Level

High school students used the technology lab during 1994 to build a life-size flight simulator. Thus, the curriculum in technology is articulated from kindergarten through the 12th grade. During the past 2 years, middle and high school students have worked, through teleconferences, with technicians at NASA and Rockwell International to build the flight simulator and a model car.

Students also use cameras and video equipment in the technology lab to contribute to their learning. In the primary grades, the pupils use Fotoman™ cameras to take still pictures, learn to project the images onto the computer monitor, and print pictures that are included in a newspaper that they take home to parents. Upper-elementary students use the video camera to do similar but more advanced things; they take still shots from the video and print them as part of projects and reports or include them in their portfolios.

The students in Ten Sleep have become computer literate and have learned to use technology as an adjunct to learning. Another important outcome for the students in this small community is the realization that the world is also a small place. For children living in the Big Horn Basin, it is easy to think that they exist for themselves and their neighbors; there are tendencies to believe that what goes on in the world does not affect them directly and to doubt that they in turn could affect someone outside of their immediate environment.

However, computer and video technology have brought the world to Ten Sleep and vice versa. With this technology, Ten Sleep students are able to reach out to others throughout their state, the nation, and the world. Teachers are now in the beginning stages of a communication project with pupils in Russia; pupils in Ten Sleep also communicate via technology with students in other parts of Wyoming and the nation.

High school graduates who go on to postsecondary education have found that their skills with technology have helped them tremendously in their college work. Other students have been able to get jobs where they can use their technological skills to their advantage.

The Effect of Technology on
Faculty Members and the Community

The technology program has also opened up a whole new world for the faculty members in Ten Sleep. Mostly veteran teachers, they have responded flexibly to the use of technology in their classroom instruction. Parents, grandparents, and community members have been involved as volunteers with pupils to implement the technology in the classroom. The technology lab is open to the public several times during the year so that the community can take advantage of the laboratory that the students use.

The success of the technology lab has made the Ten Sleep district visible throughout Wyoming. Visitors come from all over the state to find out how the district is doing it; in effect, the district has become a showcase for technology for the state. During the past two summers, Ten Sleep has offered a summer camp for Wyoming teachers and teachers from surrounding states, giving them the opportunity to learn how they might incorporate technology into their schools.

The Ten Sleep faculty members have taken advantage of the visitors to glean from them how they might improve the quality of their programs. A camp has also been offered for students during the summer; in 1995, students from the surrounding region will be able to attend a technology camp in Ten Sleep.

One important thing that the faculty members have learned is that technology changes very rapidly. They know that they have to keep current and be open to new advances; they have also learned that they need a plan to rotate old equipment out of the laboratory and replace it with technology that is likely to be more flexible in its applications. They have learned that they can learn from the students; often, students have more time to spend on technology than the teachers do. Teachers, parents, and volunteers have learned that they don't have to have all the answers to student questions; rather, adults have learned to work with the students to help them find the answers.

The technology laboratory at Ten Sleep High School has indeed brought the outside world to the students in that rural community. And in turn, its exciting program has brought educators from throughout Wyoming and its adjoining states to this small rural community. Because of an effective use of technology, life, schooling, and careers have been expanded in this rural environment. With creative leadership, collaborative efforts in small communities can develop truly effective curricu. for all grade levels—Ten Sleep has accomplished that!

SUMMARY

The quality of education in most school districts is judged by student performance on standardized tests of academic achievement; however, these focus on low-level cognitive skills that do not reflect the goals of most school districts. Schools typically want more authentic measures of student achievement but widely accepted ways of measuring these outcomes are not yet available. Thus, school districts must demonstrate effective student achievement on conventional tests while preparing parents and the public for newer methods of student assessment.

The program Monitoring Achievement in Pittsburgh (MAP) was useful in assisting teachers to ensure that students master the tool skills of learning. The advantage of achievement monitoring is that students, parents, teachers, and administrators know where students are on the continuum of learning. A syllabus examination program illustrates how a district can go beyond the basics and use a European type of examination to raise the level of expectation for student achievement.

Alternative assessment is demonstrated by the program Arts PROPEL, which develops a portfolio culture in the classroom. Students use portfolios and journals as they grow in their powers of perception and reflection in the development of products.

School districts create special programs to enhance student achievement for both college-bound and non-college-bound students. Pittsburgh's Business and Finance Academy and Public Safety Academy are examples of programs that capture the interest of students and prepare them for careers in those fields.

The multicultural education program in Pittsburgh provides educational experiences for all students to develop awareness of and respect for one another's cultures. In addition, programs are designed to help children from minority groups develop an enhanced view of their own culture while promoting the pursuit of academic goals.

The rural districts of Presque Isle, Maine, and Ten Sleep, Wyoming, demonstrate how rural communities can further the learning of their students. Presque Isle High School was not satisfied with the performance of their students on the Maine state assessment test. The faculty and administration implemented a process approach to writing; they provided a number of computer laboratories where students learn to write on word processors. This experience dramatically improved students' results on the state's assessment test in writing.

The mountain basin community of Ten Sleep, Wyoming, developed a technology laboratory for students from primary grades through high school to connect their students with the outside world. Students have learned to use computers as an adjunct to learning, working with scientists at NASA and Rockwell International and using video and computer technology to enrich their knowledge of all related subjects. The entire community of Ten Sleep has joined with the school to develop and implement what has become a model for Wyoming and surrounding states.

Note

1. Arts PROPEL materials may be obtained by contacting Harvard Project Zero, 323 Longfellow Hall, Cambridge, MA 02138.

10

Promoting Professional Development

The superintendent has a serious responsibility for the continuing professional development of teachers, administrators, and support staff in the district. I believe that the quality of instruction offered to children and youth will be largely determined by the climate of professional development. If there is no pressure on professionals to continue to improve their performance, the quality of education for students will suffer. Individual teachers and administrators may pursue their own development through studies at colleges and universities; however, the district as a whole will not thrive unless a comprehensive plan for professional improvement is in place.

Ample evidence demonstrates that typical in-service programs offered by many school districts are highly ineffective. One-day workshops for teachers and administrators do little to change behavior; at best, they can be entertaining and generate enthusiasm—enthusiasm that will die quickly without systematic follow-through. At worst, 1-day workshops can be boring, irrelevant, and a waste of time and money.

A comprehensive long-range professional development plan requires strong leadership from the superintendent. The plan needs a tight focus and a multiyear design; the inclusion of sustained follow-through to ensure an effect on the behaviors of teachers and administrators is paramount. In addition, every initiative undertaken for professional development needs to be perceived by the participants as related to previous activities (Wallace, 1993).

In this chapter, several award-winning programs created and implemented in the Pittsburgh Public Schools are reviewed. Emphasis is placed on programs designed to improve the educational leadership skills of principals and teacher renewal experiences in the teacher centers. Exemplary programs in a rural and a suburban school district, whose goals are consistent with the theory and practice described in this book, will also be briefly reviewed.

The Professional Development Priority in Pittsburgh

At the beginning of my superintendency in Pittsburgh in 1980, the board of education adopted the improvement of the quality of personnel evaluation as a priority; this set the stage for creating a professional development program for teachers and principals. The program was based on the premise that a sound evaluation system has to be based on a clear set of expectations for teachers and principals, followed by a training program to assure the district that its professionals can perform in a manner consistent with the expectations.

The first step was to convene a task force of professionals to plan a program for principals, which included principals, teachers, union leadership, and central office personnel. I reminded them that the data from the 1980 needs assessment survey clearly demonstrated that all stakeholders perceived the need to improve personnel evaluation.

There was no question in my mind that principals' evaluations of teachers had to be the first issue addressed. For principals to evaluate teachers effectively, they have to be able to observe and confer with teachers to improve instruction. All principals in Pennsylvania are required to take a course in personnel supervision; however, most Pittsburgh principals had little training in observing and conferring with teachers.

The Task Force on Professional Development filed its report with the board in late spring 1981. It recommended that the board hire a staff development team composed of four full-time trainers and a director. It also recommended that the district training program for principals focus on observing and conferring with teachers to improve instruction using

Madeline Hunter's model (1976). This recommendation was the first element in a program to prepare principals to be educational leaders. The board approved the recommendations, and four staff development trainers were hired to initiate the program in the fall of 1981.

As superintendent, I kept a close working relationship with the director of staff development and the team. Because a great deal was at stake with this program, I wanted to be involved with its development and implementation. I participated in training sessions with principals to impress on them the importance of this program to the school district.

For more than a decade, I met systematically with the staff development team to review and respond to their annual plans to improve the performance of professionals. This communicated to the team and to the district that I considered professional development of teachers and principals as one of my most important responsibilities.

PRISM I: Observing and Conferring to Improve Instruction

Pittsburgh's professional development program was named PRISM (Pittsburgh's Research-Based Instructional Supervisory Model). All professional development bore the PRISM label to let teachers and administrators know that the program was a fully integrated one.

PRISM I focused on principals' supervisory skill development. Hunter's (1976) effective teaching skills and conferring models were used to provide a common language regarding instruction for all principals. A 30-hour training program was implemented during the 1981-82 school year. All principals were trained in the following four elements of the Hunter model:

1. Selecting an objective at the correct level of difficulty
2. Teaching to an objective
3. Monitoring the progress of the learner and adjusting the teaching
4. Using, without abusing, certain principles of learning

Principals were also trained to observe instruction, take anecdotal records of their observations, and plan and conduct a conference with teachers.

This training for principals took place in peer groups with opportunities to (a) teach using elements of the Hunter model, (b) be observed by their colleagues, and (c) participate in a feedback conference. They were also coached in observing and conferring skills in their home schools.

The principals were asked to select teachers in their buildings who would be willing to allow the principals to practice their observing and conferring skills. By the end of the first year, principals were generally well versed in models of effective instruction and in observing and conferring with teachers.

The district launched its first annual Summer Principals Academy in 1982, a special summer school in which principals and vice principals taught students from grades 2 through 12 in a special 2-week program. The session was designed, in part, to refine the basic observing and conferring skills of the principals and to expand the types of teacher conferences used to improve instruction. The 1983 Summer Academy officially launched PRISM II, whose purpose was to begin training principals as educational leaders.

PRISM II: The Principal as an Educational Leader

After a year of training in observing and conferring with teachers, principals were expected to train the faculty in their own buildings using the Hunter model of effective instructional techniques. The staff development team provided resource materials and helped principals design training sessions for teachers. The fact that principals had taught students and had been observed added considerable credibility to their efforts to train their faculty members.

PRISM II was a decade-long initiative to enhance the educational leadership role of principals. Principals received training in interpreting and using data from standardized tests to identify strengths and weaknesses of students; then, they were trained to use these data in formulating plans with their faculty members to improve the performance of their students. In addition, principals were trained to use MAP data to analyze the increasing competence of students and to monitor instructional processes carefully.

By 1985, the district began to move toward site-based decision making focused on instruction. Instructional cabinets were formed in each school, designed to involve the principal and key faculty members in deciding how the educational program in the school could be improved. It was through the instructional cabinets that the principals were expected to provide strong leadership; the training prepared principals to engage teachers in shared decision making. Training programs included consensus decision making, conflict resolution, conducting effective meetings, and the like.

But the focus was on instructional improvement, not the general management of a school.

The decision to focus on the role of instructional cabinets and their role in improving the quality of education for students was deliberate. The literature on site-based decision making led us to conclude that we did not want principals and teachers to get bogged down in school management decisions and we did not want them to ignore educational issues. The literature convinced us that engaging teachers in site-based decisions that focused on administrative decisions both (a) frustrated teachers and (b) contributed to the lack of an educational focus. Thus, we concentrated on empowering teachers and principals to make the most important professional decisions: those dealing with educational programs for students.

PRISM II provided principals approximately 30 hours of training during each school year to enhance their educational leadership skills. Summer academies offered additional training as part of their professional work year. Educational leadership responsibilities became the most important part of the job description and became the major focus for performance evaluations.

As the summer academies evolved, the programs were designed by the staff development team in collaboration with a committee of principals and included both mandatory and elective sessions. The district's supervisors and principals offered minicourses based on annual needs assessment surveys administered to the principals.

Mandatory sessions focused on district priorities or issues about which all principals needed to be informed, such as "closing the racial achievement gap" and "cooperative learning."

Elective sessions allowed principals to pursue topics of interest to them, such as "strategies for managing behavior problems in the classroom" and "stress management." The staff development team kept transcripts of the principals' elective choices so that (a) the district had a record of those sessions that were popular and (b) the principals had a record of their own professional development.

PRISM III: The Schenley High School Teacher Center

The Schenley High School Teacher Center was designated as PRISM III to communicate (a) its relationship to PRISM I and II and (b) a holistic approach to professional development. This program came to have high national and international visibility as a comprehensive staff development program for secondary teachers. It won several awards for innovative programming and the use of data to inform decision making.

The Schenley program emerged from three priorities that the board of education had voted for in January 1981: improving academic achievement of students, improving the quality of personnel evaluation, and managing enrollment decline (see Chapter 7 for data relating to high school closings).

The teacher center was designed to address both student achievement and personnel evaluation. I suggested that we give all secondary teachers an 8-week, full-time, minisabbatical as a means of upgrading their instructional skills to move toward improving student achievement. The board authorized me to develop plans for their review.

I recommended Schenley High School as the site for the teacher center for three reasons. First, at the time, it was the lowest-achieving high school in the city, and I wanted to do something to improve the quality of education for those students. Second, it was a school whose student population was 87% African American; I wanted to integrate it by establishing magnet programs within the school that would attract white students. Third, it was located close to the central administrative offices where we had easy access to it.

General Planning for the Schenley Center

To begin, I made presentations to all the high school faculties regarding the purposes of the teacher center. I invited them to join planning groups to design the center's general characteristics; over 200 teachers volunteered. More than a dozen committees were formed to develop recommendations for the board on issues such as how the faculty would be selected, the types of programs to be offered to teachers, and how the center would be integrated into an operating high school. I gave these committees three design criteria: (a) the experience had to be clinical—teachers would have to observe their peers, engage in the analysis of instruction, teach for clinical resident teachers, and receive feedback on their teaching; (b) there had to be content update experiences so that the participants were knowledgeable about the most recent trends and research in their academic disciplines; and (c) there had to be a focus on the needs of adolescents so that teachers would understand the social forces operating and be prepared to work with students more effectively to reduce the dropout rate.

The planning committees worked for 6 months to develop general recommendations for the board. In June 1982, the board approved the plans for the Schenley High School Teacher Center and detailed planning started for the opening of the center in September 1983. The Ford Foundation funded this first year of intensive planning as well as evaluative research over the next 6 years to document (a) the implementation process and (b) the effect of the center experience on faculty and students (Wallace, LeMahieu, & Bickel, 1990).

The Pittsburgh Federation of Teachers (PFT) agreed contractually to designate Schenley as a school of special status, thus allowing the school to close and then reopen with new faculty. Three categories of teachers composed the Schenley High School Teacher Center: (a) *clinical resident teachers,* to mentor visiting teachers and coach them to improve pedagogy; (b) *demonstration teachers,* to show specific techniques for visiting teachers; and (c) *visiting teachers,* who attended the center for a renewal experience. Approximately 200 teachers applied for the positions of clinical resident teachers or demonstration teachers for Schenley.

A fourth category of teachers was called *replacement teachers*; they were selected and trained to take the place of the teachers being released from the high schools to attend the center.

A committee of 75 secondary teachers volunteered to work with the center administration in developing the detailed plans for the center's opening. The first group of teachers to attend were the replacement teachers; we wanted to be sure that they would fulfill the district's expectations for instruction so that principals and parents could be reasonably satisfied that students were receiving competent instruction while their regular teachers attended the teacher center.

Clinical resident teachers taught half-time; the rest of the time they worked with visiting teachers and conducted seminars on special topics. Fifty visiting teachers spent 8 weeks at the center, during which they had the following experiences:

> They received training in effective instructional techniques, practiced those techniques, observed peers' teaching, and provided feedback to them.
>
> They observed clinical resident teachers teach students at Schenley, taught those students themselves, and received feedback on their teaching.
>
> They attended seminars in their academic disciplines and on topics dealing with today's adolescents.
>
> If they chose, they participated in externships with business, industries, and universities; these experiences provided opportunities

to view how their academic disciplines were applied in the work world or higher education.

Visiting teachers had individual plans for what they would focus on during the center experience. In addition, when they left the center, they had a follow-up plan to extend their center experiences. These preparation and follow-through plans were developed in collaboration with the center administration. Principals were expected to provide opportunities for teachers to observe one another after they returned from the center so they could continue to develop the skills they had gained.

The Schenley Center was designed to have a 5-year life span. Therefore, from 1983 to 1988, all secondary teachers in the district were provided a renewal experience. The Schenley Phase II program was implemented to offer all high schools opportunities to develop proposals to follow up on the Schenley experience; each high school could plan and implement an innovative program that would continue professional development and improve the quality of education for students.

The Schenley High School Teacher Center was so successful that suburban school districts in the Pittsburgh area asked if they could send their teachers to the program. We pilot tested the program with two teachers from a suburban community and found it to be equally relevant for them. From 1989 to 1991, the Schenley Center offered a tuition program for suburban teachers; newly hired teachers for Pittsburgh secondary schools also attended the center during this period. The center closed in June 1991.

PRISM IV: The Brookline
Elementary Teacher Center

The Schenley Center created a very positive climate for teacher professionalism in the Pittsburgh schools; therefore, I met with the leadership of the PFT to inquire if they would collaborate on a teacher center for the elementary schools. They were interested. The union contract required the board to have 50 school-based spare teachers on hand at the beginning of each school year to serve in the absence of regular teachers. I proposed that we use these 50 as the replacements needed to release full-time teachers to attend the center. The PFT agreed to this proposal; subsequently, it was included in the contract, which allowed us to open an elementary teacher center.

The Brookline Elementary School Teacher Center opened in September 1985 after a 6-month planning period. The program was modeled after the Schenley program with some important differences. In the planning process, the elementary teachers decided that they did not want to be away from their regular classrooms for an 8-week period as had their secondary counterparts. They decided on a 5-week program focusing on developing language proficiency in children and observing and conferring to improve instruction.

As with the Schenley Center, the PFT agreed to close the school and reopen it as a school of special status. Thus, teachers throughout the city could apply for positions as clinical resident and demonstration teachers. The school was staffed with the district's most outstanding teachers to provide a stimulating renewal program for the district's elementary teachers.

PRISM V: The Greenway Middle School Teacher Center

In 1987, the Greenway Middle School Teacher Center opened. Once again, the program was modeled after the Schenley and Brookline programs but had unique characteristics that reflected the needs of teachers dealing with early adolescents.

One important difference occurred with the Greenway model. All middle school teachers in the city were organized into interdisciplinary instructional teams by grade level. The Greenway plan called for the teams to be brought intact to the center for their renewal experiences. The middle school teachers who engaged in the yearlong planning for Greenway decided on a 7-week program, and the primary focus was on growth and development of the early adolescent and instructional strategies consistent with the characteristics of this age group.

As with Schenley and Brookline, the PFT agreed to close Greenway and create a school of special status so that we could staff it with the district's most outstanding middle school teachers. Staffing patterns were similar to Schenley and Brookline regarding clinical resident and demonstration teachers. The replacement teacher group was composed of half of the school-based spare teachers. Thus, both Greenway and Brookline Teacher Centers had 25 replacement teachers to release regular classroom teachers to attend their respective centers.

The Effect of the Teacher Centers in Pittsburgh

The teacher center program influenced the quality of education in Pittsburgh both directly and indirectly. One focus of the program was to improve the ability of teachers to use higher-order questioning. A study completed at the Schenley Center involved observing teachers in their classrooms prior to coming to the center and after their return. The results indicated that teachers who received training in formulating and asking higher-order questions used this technique more frequently after the training. The use of these questioning techniques was consistent with the district's effort to improve the critical thinking ability of students (see Chapter 9).

The centers had a very important influence on the development of teacher and principal professionalism in the Pittsburgh schools. The programs were designed by teachers for the teachers of the district and delivered by teachers in the district and by our staff development team. The centers drew on the most competent teachers in the city to engage their peers in an intensive professional development experience. The centers were instrumental in developing a great sense of pride in the city schools as hundreds of visitors came from around the country and the world to learn about our comprehensive professional development program.

The teacher centers also paved the way for developing the role of *instructional teacher leader* that became an important centerpiece of the Professionalism and Education Partnership (PEP). This partnership became the vehicle for the administration, PFT, and the Administrators Association to forge ahead with the continuing professional development of teachers and administrators in the Pittsburgh Schools (see Chapter 7 for a detailed presentation).

The Schenley High School Teacher Center also had important outcomes for students. As a result of the successful implementation of international studies and high technology magnet programs, the school grew to over 1,100 pupils and by 1992 was racially integrated. Also by 1992, Schenley was the second ranking academic high school in the city. Thus, two important goals for students were reached as a result of the teacher center.

Professional Development in Multicultural Education

In 1989, the Pittsburgh Public Schools initiated a multicultural education program to address the issues of minority student achievement; the program was designed, in part, to ensure that faculty members had the appropriate skills, attitudes, and dispositions to effectively teach African American students. One of the forces motivating this initiative was the need to face the racial achievement gap between the district's African American and white students.

The initiative directly addressed the educational needs of students with a multicultural curriculum; a substantial effort was also made to enable teachers to deal effectively with minority students and the new curriculum. One of the key strategies in the multicultural program was training teachers to identify student learning styles and adjust instruction accordingly. The district selected the Prospect Middle School as the site to create a model of multicultural education that would ultimately be disseminated to all district schools. It was chosen because it was perceived by the community and the district as a troubled school; it had a record of low achievement and was located in a white neighborhood that did not fully accept the district's desegregation plan that bused African American students to the school.

It was renamed the Prospect Multicultural Center, and its goal was to demonstrate a climate in which all students' cultures could be appreciated, thus improving the students' behavior and academic achievement. From the teachers' perspective, major emphasis was placed on honoring the cultural differences of the student body; teachers were prepared to infuse genuine multicultural knowledge into the curriculum and acquire the skills to address the learning styles of students. The program also trained students in conflict resolution and cooperative learning and eliminated academic tracking.

In evaluating the Prospect Multicultural Center, researchers Nettles et al. (1994) from Johns Hopkins University observed that the progress made during the initial 3 years was mixed. Their perceptions regarding professional development were summarized as follows:

> We might start by understanding that organizations tend to do most what they do best. Staff development and the establishment of innovative practices in schools are the hallmarks of the Pittsburgh Public Schools. In the present program they excelled in these areas. But, there were fewer signs of progress in other areas. (p. 158)

By 1991, the board of education decided to close the teacher centers and deploy the financial resources to the multicultural program and an early childhood initiative. Currently, the multicultural program is organized to deliver a program of "equity and excellence" that has as its primary goal helping schools achieve the goals of equitable and excellent learning outcomes for all pupils. Components of the program include the following:

Cultural influences on the learner

Learning styles and teaching strategies

Equitable assessment

Cooperative learning

Observing for equity

Multicultural curricula infusion

Staff development personnel and replacement teachers move into a school to provide teachers with a 4-week multicultural education training program. Replacement teachers release the school faculty from their teaching assignments and the staff development team delivers the training. This school-based approach that brings training to the teachers is the current mode for professional development in the Pittsburgh schools.

Professional Development
in Rural and Suburban Communities

Exemplary programs in rural Kansas and suburban Maryland have incorporated initiatives similar to those used in Pittsburgh, yet they also bring different perspectives to staff development.

Royal Valley Public Schools,
Mayetta, Kansas: Results-Based Staff Development

Two small towns with a total of 878 students are served by the Royal Valley Public Schools in Mayetta, Kansas. The superintendent, a former director of curriculum and staff development in another Kansas school district, facilitates a comprehensive staff development program for this rural school district (M. Reilly, personal communication, February 3, 1995). The most powerful approach for rural communities is to form a consortium with other school districts where staff members can make connections with other teachers at the same grade level or discipline. Individually, small school districts have very limited resources for professional development. By pooling financial and human resources, the consortium is able to provide professional development programs for teachers that would not otherwise be possible; thus, this is the format most frequently used.

Regional Consortium

Two of the major foci of the program in recent years have been a writing project and an performance assessment project. Following the model of state testing, the writing project focuses on a six-trait analytic writing assessment model for students in Grades 5, 7, and 10 in all districts. One hundred teachers from the regional consortium were trained by staff from the Northwest Evaluation Association in Portland, Oregon, to rate student writing.

Twelve teachers, two from each of the six school districts, were prepared as teacher trainers for their respective districts during each of the past 2 years. They were trained to offer professional development for teachers in process writing techniques related to the six specified traits.

Through the use of computers, the performance assessment program linked teachers in the consortium who were interested in authentic assessment. They are able to share with each other the performance assessments developed in their classrooms. Each district in the consortium has a team of three teachers and a principal who oversee the program. Principals are more directly involved in the assessment program, as opposed to the writing program, so they take more direct responsibility for the project.

Results-Based Staff Development

Perhaps the most innovative practice in Royal Valley, and unique to the district, is the results-based staff development program. This recently developed program gives teachers credit toward salary increases when they can demonstrate application of techniques learned through professional development. Credit can be earned at four levels: *individual participation, evidence of implementation, evidence of student effect,* and *leadership responsibilities.* At the participation level, a teacher can earn credits by sharing techniques learned in workshops or through reading; at the implementation level, the teacher shows, and a building team validates, that instructional practices have been successfully implemented. The student effect level requires the teacher to demonstrate that, by using new instructional techniques, more students are more successful based on criteria established by the building team. At the leadership level, the teacher earns credit by training or coaching peers in effective instructional techniques resulting in improved student learning performance.

This results-oriented staff development puts a premium on action taken by teachers to improve the quality of education for their own pupils—at the student effect level. It also provides opportunities for teachers to pursue collegial professional development as a means of earning credits needed for certification and salary increments. This performance-based program is gaining much attention in Kansas and is clearly an innovative practice that places a premium on student learning outcomes as the proper focus for professional development programs.

Montgomery County, Maryland: A Comprehensive Staff Development Program

Montgomery County, Maryland, is a large suburban school district outside Washington, D.C., with 180 schools, 118,000 students, 7,000 teachers, and 473 administrators. It is well known as having one of the most comprehensive staff development programs in the country. I will describe only two of the many current initiatives: one emphasizing decentralized staff development and the other centralized staff development for preparing principals.

Decentralized Staff Development: The School Improvement Unit

In 1992, the Montgomery County Schools Staff Development Program, which had existed since the 1980s, was restructured into two units to reflect changed priorities and reduced budget allocations. Currently, staff development is organized through a systemwide training unit providing training for teachers, administrators, and support staff. A school improvement unit offers technical support to enable the schools to implement their own staff development programs based on the needs of individual schools (K. Blumsack, personal communication, February 18, 1995).

The School Improvement Unit (SIU). The mission of this team is to provide schools with the assistance needed to reach the goals established by the schools rather than the districtwide initiatives. It works with schools to identify available training materials on a particular topic (e.g., sexual harassment); the unit also helps pull together the materials needed for training teachers, administrators, and community groups. The unit is connected to the Office of Instruction so that both groups can draw from the shared resources.

The emphasis of the SIU is twofold: (a) helping schools be successful with their own vision of schooling and (b) helping schools implement priorities established by the board. For example, the county currently has a districtwide emphasis on the improvement of student achievement in writing, math, and science. The unit responds to schools who ask for help in implementing such innovations as electronic portfolios and event-based science. The unit also examines school improvement plans throughout the district, identifies trends in those plans, and creates pertinent districtwide training events. The SIU demonstrates a bottom-up approach to staff development that emphasizes helping schools actualize their own visions for school effectiveness.

Faculty obtain staff development training in any of three ways: by attending systemwide events, through SIU on-site training, or by joining teachers from other schools who have similar training needs. Schools are responsible for examining their own data to determine the needs of their pupils; SIUs within each school are responsible for analyzing their own information and gathering additional survey data to develop their improvement plans.

Each school has an allocation for staff development from the district based on its number of professional staff. The amount ranges from $2,700 to $8,000, depending on staff size. Schools may spend money on substitute teachers to release staff for development work, send teachers to conferences, hire consultants, and so forth. The schools do not pay for the training services provided by the SIU.

A major emphasis in current staff development training is to ensure that the new skills are used immediately in the classroom. For example, some of the training currently available through global access and technology integration use action research projects specifically related to technology used in classrooms. These programs are individualized for the teachers, and results are seen in the classrooms within a few days; teachers being trained in technology integration also receive coaching and additional support to assist direct classroom application.

Centralized Staff Development:
The Systemwide Training Unit (STU)

The STU has as its responsibility the major systemwide training of classified staff, new teachers, and administrators; it is also responsible for establishing partnerships with colleges and universities to support the training of professionals (K. Rohr, personal communication, February 25, 1995).

Principal selection and training. A comprehensive principal identification and training program has been operating in the Montgomery County Schools since 1970; the program described here has been in operation since 1983. Initially, the district used its own principal assessment program to identify potential school leaders. Currently, aspiring principals must (a) complete state certification requirements, (b) pass the National Association of Secondary School Principals (NASSP) Assessment offered by the Maryland State Department of Education, (c) go through a screening and interview process, and (d) be selected to participate in the training program, which is based on the four goals of the district:

- Ensuring success for every student
- Providing effective instructional programs
- Strengthening partnerships in education, business, and communities
- Creating a positive work environment in a self-renewing organization

The program trains assistant principals for secondary schools and principals for elementary schools. I will describe only the elementary principals' training program.

Elementary principal training options. Training that may lead to an elementary principalship comes in two forms: *acting assistant principal* or *principal trainee.* Ideally, the candidate can participate in a 2-year program by acting as an assistant elementary principal for 1 year and then serving as a trainee for an additional year; the two programs, however, are not necessarily sequential, nor is it necessary to take both programs to become an elementary principal.

The acting assistant principalship is designed to give a candidate basic experience in administration and training to prepare him or her for the principalship. The trainee program is highly selective; a candidate may be chosen to enter the trainee program and bypass the assistant principalship experience. The candidate for a principalship, however, must successfully complete either the trainee program or the acting assistant principal program.

Once selected, the acting assistant principal can engage in training but is given no promise of employment either as a trainee or eventual principal. On the other hand, a trainee is chosen because of outstanding potential and in all likelihood will be appointed as a principal soon after completion of a yearlong program. Both groups are provided with very specific training on a variety of topics that will prepare them for the demanding role of an elementary principal in Montgomery County.

If a candidate is selected to be a trainee, he or she is specifically trained in leadership skills, curriculum, policies and procedures, and facilitation skills during the summer prior to the traineeship. During the yearlong program, he or she is given additional training conducted by principals. The trainee begins by shadowing the principal and gradually taking on responsibilities; after 6 months, the principal leaves the building for 2 to 3 months to allow the trainee to lead and manage the school. The released principal uses the time to provide a service for the district and engage in personal renewal activities.

In addition to on-the-job training and mentoring, the trainee enrolls in district workshops on issues and topics such as school law, group dynamics, negotiating skills, special needs programs, fiscal accountability, enrichment and instructional strategies, interpersonal skills, visioning, role of the principal in the 21st century, effective writing, school safety, supervision of teachers and support staff, and many more. These are presented by outstanding practitioners throughout the year. The trainee also participates in the ongoing professional development program provided to new and experienced principals.

One of the most unique and valuable features of the trainee program is the monthly supervisory team meeting to provide assistance and mentoring. The supervisory team is composed of an associate or deputy superintendent, a director from the Office of School Administration, an outside consultant who is a retired district principal, a representative from the STU, and the school principal trainer. Once a month, the trainee meets with this team for a series of prescribed activities, such as a review of the highlights of what the trainee has experienced. For each seminar, the trainee selects one leadership situation in which he or she has been involved and analyzes it for the supervisory team. The team engages in discussion by probing, providing different perspectives on the situation, and coaching the trainee as to alternative courses of action. This high-powered supervisory group provides invaluable insight and feedback to the trainee that could not be duplicated in a conventional training program.

Principals tend to stay in touch with their trainees and continue to be mentors. The trainee experience contributes to a spirit of professionalism that permeates the career of the trainee; it also contributes to high professional expectations for the administrators of Montgomery County.

The district usually has between 10 and 14 trainees per year based on the number of projected principalship vacancies. After successful completion of the program, trainees are placed on the promotion eligibility list. They may then be interviewed for vacancies using a structured interview process that involves school staff and community members. Successful interviewees are nominated for the principalships.

Partnerships for professional development. In addition to the extensive ongoing professional development program for principals, the district has developed partnerships with many colleges and universities for continuing education of professional staff. A special partnership with Johns Hopkins University offers master's degree programs in educational administration, which provides the district with a steady stream of candidates with master's degrees who are ready to be considered for the pool of potential principals.

The changing demographics of the Montgomery County district, the steady growth of its diverse student population, and the parents' concerns for a high quality of education create a culture of high expectations. The district has responded with an exceptionally comprehensive and high-quality program to assist its professionals and support staff to create a positive work environment in a self-renewing organization. The district is to be commended for providing such valuable opportunities for its employees.

SUMMARY

School districts need to keep their professionals on the cutting edge of reform to support effective school renewal. The superintendent is responsible for overseeing the development and implementation of a comprehensive plan for continuing professional development of teachers and administrators.

PRISM is the vehicle for professional development in Pittsburgh. PRISM I and II focused on increasing the instructional leadership skills of principals with an emphasis on observing and conferring with teachers to improve instruction. PRISM III, IV, and V created teacher centers that released teachers from their regular duties to engage in 5- to 8-week renewal experiences. Teachers designed the center programs and the most competent teachers in the district took faculty positions at the centers as clinical resident teachers.

The multicultural and early childhood programs in Pittsburgh now bring professional development teams to schools to engage teachers in training activities.

The Royal Valley School District in Mayetta, Kansas, demonstrates how a rural school district can combine resources with surrounding districts to provide professional development activities that it could not otherwise afford. Royal Valley uses a results-based staff development program. Teachers earn credit toward salary advancement when they demonstrate that they use skills in the classroom learned in staff development; the program also gives credit to teachers who show that new techniques have an effect on pupil learning. Teachers also earn credit when they train or coach their peers in new techniques that improve student learning.

Montgomery County, Maryland, has one of the most comprehensive professional development programs in the country. Its schools are now responsible for conducting their own needs assessments and designing initiatives to address their priorities. An SIU assists schools to design their own professional development programs. Schools also have their own discretionary staff development funds to help actualize their vision: They may also join with other district schools to address their needs in a bottom-up approach to staff development.

The STU provides an exceptionally comprehensive program for professional and support staff. The principal training program is particularly effective. Teachers may participate in two programs that prepare them for the principalship. The acting assistant principal program prepares teachers with basic training for the role. The highly selective principal trainee program provides special workshops and a monthly supervisory team meeting; in the team meeting, the trainee receives valuable feedback on specific situations in which he or she has been involved. The principal trainee and the school improvement programs are only two examples of the extensive staff development programs in a dynamic school district.

11

Engaging the Community in Reform Initiatives

The superintendent must enlist the help of the district's stakeholders in developing the vision and initiatives of the excellence agenda. The reasons are twofold: (a) to develop a constituency for the vision and the excellence agenda and (b) to build a constituency for the financial support of the agenda and the strategic plan.

To illustrate the engagement of staff and community, the work of two task forces in Pittsburgh that significantly influenced education in the district are described. The first was a task force for magnet schools initiated in the years prior to my arrival as superintendent in 1980. It significantly affected the design of a desegregation plan that was approved by the board of education and subsequently accepted by the Pennsylvania Human Relations Commission in settlement of a desegregation case. The second was a task force on school restructuring that I initiated just prior to my retirement in 1992. It set the stage for the implementation of a plan that would prepare the district for the 21st century.

To illustrate the building of constituencies for financial support of a district, I describe school-business partnerships in Pittsburgh and outstanding community involvement in Tupelo, Mississippi, and Palatine, Illinois.

The Magnet School Planning Task Force

The board of education and the district's staff had been wrestling with desegregation plans in Pittsburgh from the mid-1960s through 1979. During this period, the board judged as unacceptable all the alternative plans developed by the staff.

To assist in the development of a voluntary magnet program, the superintendent and board invited the executive director of the Allegheny Conference on Community Development to head a task force of parents, community members, and district staff to design and propose a plan. The Allegheny conference is a prestigious organization that deals with public affairs and is composed of chief executive officers of major corporations in the city. Thus, with the conference's executive director leading the magnet school task force planning, significant attention would be paid to its recommendations.

The magnet plan focused primarily on elementary and middle schools in the east end of Pittsburgh, an upper-middle-class, white community where many children attended private schools. The plan proposed several options for parents at the elementary school level, including international studies academies in French, German, Spanish, and Italian; open education schools; and traditional academies. Magnet middle schools included a classical academy, a creative and performing arts academy, a traditional academy, and an international studies academy. At the secondary level, a creative and performing arts high school and a traditional academy were open. In addition, schools-within-schools programs were offered in some secondary schools.

By late 1979, the board agreed to implement both a mandatory plan and a magnet plan to accomplish desegregation. Part of the mandatory plan called for busing students to the district's middle schools to achieve racial balance. Selected contiguous elementary schools were also realigned to meet desegregation guidelines.

Several parents and community members filed a suit with the Pennsylvania Human Relations Commission alleging that the desegregation plan was inadequate. When I arrived as superintendent in September 1980, the case was in the courts awaiting a decision. When a decision was rendered in 1982, the court accepted the board's plan but insisted that the district address needs in additional elementary and secondary schools in specific areas of the city.

By spring 1982, the magnet school program was working very well and was perceived positively by parents and the general public. To address the issues presented by the courts, I recommended the expansion of the voluntary desegregation plan, particularly at the secondary school level. Three of these schools were of concern to the courts because of racial imbalance. Through the Pennsylvania Human Relations Commission, the court accepted the opening of a vocational high school and the creation of high technology and international studies programs in another to further desegregate the schools. The initial work of the magnet school task force had laid the groundwork for both the successful implementation of magnet schools and the desegregation program. The magnet programs improved the quality of education and the quality of options for students and voluntarily desegregated the schools.

In addition to magnet schools, a revision of the secondary program for gifted students, developed by another task force, proved to be a powerful means of attracting white students back to the public schools. In retrospect, the magnet program did much to revitalize the Pittsburgh Public Schools and help the district maintain a stable racial population of students composed of 52% African American and 48% white students throughout the 1980s and into the 1990s.

The School Restructuring Task Force

A task force was convened in 1992 to develop a blueprint for school restructuring; the goal was to design state-of-the-art education for children and youths into the 21st century. The work of the task force was aimed at preparing staff, parents, and the general public for the changes that would be needed for 21st-century schools. It was also convened to provide communitywide advice regarding significant policy decisions to made by the board relating to restructuring. Thus, it was important to have the chief stakeholders of the schools engaged in this process.

A second restructuring effort that influenced the work of the task force was the National Alliance for School Restructuring. This is an organization of school districts and state education agencies engaged in school restructuring; they share resources and technical assistance to promote each member's goals. The district was a member, and the alliance provided information that gave another perspective on policy issues related to restructuring.

A third influence was a within-district competition in which teachers and administrators competed to design and implement plans for restructuring existing schools with private foundation and board support. A committee of community leaders and district staff rated the proposals and made recommendations to the board for awarding contracts for restructuring. As this process developed, it provided additional experience that helped to inform the development of policies for restructuring.

Subcommittees

The task force was composed of subcommittees that dealt with policy issues. They addressed issues such as curriculum, assessment of student learning, central office support, personnel recruitment, and evaluation. Each subcommittee (a) was cochaired by a community representative and a school district employee; (b) was allowed to recruit members, as needed, from the school district, the business community, and the general public, with emphasis on parents; (c) established its own meeting schedule and meeting place to facilitate its work; (d) was provided with a mission statement or charge and guiding questions to initiate their deliberations; and (e) was provided with a time line for preparation of interim and final reports.

Steering Committee

The cochairs of each subcommittee served as members of the steering committee, which provided overall guidance for the project. I assigned several members of central administration (e.g., legal counsel, personnel officer) so that they could advise the steering committee of constraints that should be considered in developing the plan. I served as chair of the steering committee until my retirement in 1992; the steering committee continued its work beyond that time. The policy issues relating to school restructuring are significant for any school district but especially so in a large urban district. If one of the goals of restructuring is to provide greater autonomy at the school level, then there are significant implications for district policy. For example, consider the following:

If individual schools are given freedom to design their own curricula to achieve specific learning outcomes, how will the district hold them accountable for general district learning outcomes?

If individual schools are allowed to recruit and recommend their own faculty and administration, how will this be accomplished given the collective bargaining agreements and state-imposed personnel eligibility requirements?

If individual schools are interested in using authentic measures of student achievement, to what extent will they be required to respond to the district's testing program?

If individual schools are to have the ability to develop and monitor their own budgets, what interface will they have with the district's budget director?

These and other issues provided the substance of discussion for individual subcommittees and the steering committee. Policy decisions adopted by the board of education have significant effects on the operation of schools throughout the city; therefore, the participation of the teachers union, the administrators association, parents, the business community, and the general public was important in the planning process.

Forums

To engage the broad community more directly, the district invited the Pittsburgh Council on Public Education (PCPE), an independent organization of parents and community members, to plan and coordinate public forums. PCPE had a 25-year history of promoting the Pittsburgh Public Schools. Although the membership of PCPE was, historically, predominantly upper-middle-class white parents, it provided an important, independent voice for the public regarding the district's affairs. The forums offered parents and community members an opportunity to state their opinions about what the district ought to consider in school restructuring plans. Information gathered from each of the forum meetings was relayed to the steering committee and the planning subcommittees. Prior to the submission of the final plan to the board of education, the forums would be reconvened to allow participants to react to and give input to the final planning documents.

The Strategic Plan

The restructuring task force work was blended into the development of the strategic plan for the Pittsburgh Public Schools following my retirement; the strategic plan was imposed on the school district by the Pennsylvania State Education Agency. Each district in the state is required to submit a plan, formulated with public participation, that (a) meets the planning criteria established by the state and (b) will be continually updated to address the issues of quality education. In December 1994 the draft of the strategic plan was delivered to all Pittsburgh households. Public forums in each of the geographic areas provided further public input to the plans for the Pittsburgh Schools.

School-Business Partnerships

In the early 1980s, school-business partnerships were formalized in the Pittsburgh Public Schools through collaboration with the Allegheny Conference on Community Development. The conference hired a director for the program to begin developing partnerships for virtually every school in the district.

The purpose of the partnerships was to build better understanding and relationships between the schools and the business community. At the time of initiation, there was some mistrust between the two. School people tended to view the business community as outspoken critics; thus, many schools were wary of developing relationships with businesses. Similarly, business people often found themselves uneasy in the presence of educators who spoke a language they did not comprehend. Business leaders were often critical of high school graduates; many employers found them lacking in the skills needed to perform effectively in the work world.

The program developed slowly over several years to the point where over 130 partnerships were developed with the 80 public schools in the city. Some schools had multiple partnerships based on specific relationships for special academic programs. Schools and businesses had to develop mutual trust before much progress could be made, and it developed more quickly with some schools than with others. Initial "getting to know you" transactions were a necessary part of trust building. Often, the initial activities were celebrations in which the businesses would provide funds to support activities for students.

Partnerships developed most effectively when the individual liaison persons in the school and the business were given sufficient time to address the tasks of the partnership. If the job of coordinating partner was an added responsibility for either party with no released time available, the relationship was slow in developing or, in some cases, did not develop at all.

Once the partnerships had eased through the initial stage, they focused on the more substantive aspects of education. The best partnerships developed around specific academic programs with strong leadership provided by both parties. Here are examples of two such programs.

The Business and Finance Academy

One of the most successful partnerships was initiated by a third-party agency. The National Urban League approached the Pittsburgh schools through the Pittsburgh Urban League to develop a partnership with the banking industry; the goal of the program was to prepare minority students for careers in banking. The Pittsburgh Urban League assigned a leadership person to oversee the partnership development, and the school district provided a director for a Business and Finance Academy at Westinghouse High School, the city's only all-African American high school.

The partnership was a major alliance between the city's banking industry and the school district. Banking representatives worked with school district and urban league personnel to design the curriculum and create a school-within-a-school program at Westinghouse High. Over several years, the banking industry offered in-service training programs for the academy teachers so that they would be fully apprised of modern banking techniques as well as the expectations that the industry had for high school graduates as entry-level employees. Summer jobs were available for students as they progressed through the educational program to better prepare them to succeed.

The program selected students judged to have academic potential but who had failed the ninth grade. These students were nurtured through a demanding program. The Urban League and school personnel created an esprit de corp to encourage students to work hard so that they could find employment in the banking industry. The program held high expectations for students; rewards, such as jackets and T-shirts, were offered when the expectations were met.

Although the program was originally designed to provide employment after high school graduation, the majority of the graduates chose to go on to higher education. The high school graduation rate for students in the program exceeded 90% of those taken into the program.

The Westinghouse Electric Partnership

The most extensive partnership the Pittsburgh Schools had during the 1980s was with the Westinghouse Electric Corporation. The two cooperated successfully on small projects during the early 1980s. During 1986, Westinghouse's centennial year, however, I pursued a more substantial partnership that would serve the needs of both institutions. Westinghouse had an aggressive affirmative action program to recruit minority scientists and engineers; yet the corporation was having difficulty meeting its goals because of the general lack of African Americans who were preparing for careers in mathematics, science, and engineering. In the settlement of the school desegregation case, the Pittsburgh school district committed to improving the quality of education in its only all-African American high school—George Westinghouse High School.

The facts that account for the successful partnership are the following:

1. The school was named in honor of the founder of Westinghouse Electric Corporation.
2. The collaboration began during the corporation's centennial year.
3. The school district proposed to develop the Science and Mathematics Academy at Westinghouse High School, a new magnet program to prepare African American students to pursue higher education in mathematics, science, and engineering.
4. The district sought the assistance of Westinghouse Electric to provide summer collegiate experiences and scholarships for students who successfully met the goals of the program.
5. The district renovated and updated all the science classrooms and laboratories with equipment and materials to operate a first-class program.
6. A parent was hired as the academy's recruitment coordinator who also made possible auxiliary services, such as transporting students to tutoring sessions.
7. Westinghouse Electric funded membership in professional organizations for academy teachers and supported their attendance at professional conferences.
8. Westinghouse Electric donated a van to the school district to transport students to university campuses for tutoring.

The Science and Mathematics Academy used the program design of New York City's Bronx High School of Science, which required the students to complete 5 years of math and science courses in 4 years. Students attended 2-week summer science programs on college campuses for 3 summers. These summer programs were designed so that students could experience college life and have learning and laboratory experiences to prepare them for the coming school year. The first summer session, at Carnegie Mellon University, orients students for studies in chemistry; the second summer, at Penn State University, prepares students to study physics; the third summer, at the University of Maryland, provides students with experiences in environmental studies. Students from Carnegie Mellon University and the University of Pittsburgh offer tutoring in math and science as needed.

The Westinghouse Electric-Pittsburgh Public Schools partnership is an example of an extensive and sophisticated relationship between a school district and a business enterprise that served the needs of both institutions. The relationship grew slowly over several years as both parties developed confidence in each other. Westinghouse Electric demonstrated that it was taking constructive action to develop a minority workforce in the field. The Pittsburgh school district could show that it was fulfilling its commitment to the courts by improving the quality of education for students at George Westinghouse High School. The Science and Mathematics Academy also enhanced the image of the high school in its own community.

Community Collaboration

The Pittsburgh New Futures Program

Broadscale community collaboration to serve the needs of children, youths, and families is a worthy goal for school districts and community agencies to pursue; however, it is a task not easily accomplished (White & Wehlage, in press). The Annie E. Casey Foundation has invested millions of dollars in a New Futures Program to promote such partnerships.

The basic goal of such collaboration is well described by Schorr (1988). Community involvement is essential if local, regional, and school district resources are to be wisely spent to ensure that children come to school ready to learn. Children and families who live in poverty face many challenges that can seriously interfere with schooling. Many receive services from several social service agencies who tend to (a) lack communication with each other, (b) duplicate services, and (c) do not see cases through to successful conclusions because of poor service coordination. The problems arise because agencies are prohibited by regulation from sharing information with one another. The schools are caught in the middle of a power struggle between the agencies for resources and information. The children and families are the losers in this turf battle. Collaboration among human service agencies is necessary to achieve more effective uses of human and financial resources for this population. Schorr (1988) also cites examples of communities that have achieved effective working relationships between human service agencies.

The Annie E. Casey Foundation's New Futures Program granted monies to five cities to initiate programs to facilitate the formation of collaboratives; Pittsburgh was one of the five. The ambitious nature of the Casey project and the growing pains experienced by both the foundation and the collaborating cities impeded progress. In Savannah, Georgia, and Pittsburgh, however, formal organizations were created that are still working to address effective community collaboration.

When the Pittsburgh New Futures Board was convened by the mayor in 1987, it was not clear that its mission was to be chief advocate for all of the children in the community; thus, the board did not include a sufficient number of key city and county leaders. The broader mission evolved as the program developed and as the Casey Foundation goals became more focused. It became apparent in Pittsburgh that to achieve the collaboration required, key leaders should formulate policies and oversee their implementation, including the mayor, the chair of the county commissioners, the superintendent of schools, the Allegheny Conference executive director, chief executive officers of Pittsburgh's corporate community, and other community leaders. Unless the chief decision makers of the community were directly involved in human resource policy development, collaboration would not succeed.

The membership of the Allegheny Conference was concerned with workforce development during the early 1990s. Some members participated in designing the Strategy 21 plan, sponsored by the Allegheny County commissioners and dealing with western Pennsylvania's workforce issues for the 21st century. The business community also supported the Goals 2000 for education supported by the Bush and Clinton administrations. A convergence of interest occurred; as a result, the boards of New Futures and the Allegheny Conference created the Allegheny Policy Council for Youth and Workforce Development to address more effectively the issues of community collaboration. In the interest of better partnership, the New Futures Board voted itself out of existence and endorsed the new policy council. The executive director of the Allegheny Conference led the planning to create the new council; formed in 1992, the council implements policies and initiatives that address community collaboration on county and regional levels. One of the goals of the policy council is to maximize the use of human and financial resources to (a) improve the quality of education and human services (b) prepare the 21st-century workforce, and (c) improve the quality of life for western Pennsylvanians.

The Pittsburgh Chamber of Commerce Collaboration

Although the theme of this book is educational leadership, I want to include a description of one management collaboration I initiated to illustrate the broad nature of community collaboration. I sought the help of the Pittsburgh Chamber of Commerce to improve the quality of school support services, such as the inefficient food service department that required a $2 million annual subsidy.

The Food Service Department

The food service problem in the Pittsburgh schools in 1980 was symbolized by a huge food service center. Built in the 1960s, the center was intended to support the district's food service program, specifically the five great city high schools to be built to house 5,000 students each. The five high schools were never built but the food service center was and it soon became a white elephant for the school district. To address this costly situation, I asked the executive director of the Pittsburgh Chamber of Commerce to convene a blue-ribbon panel to review the food service program and make recommendations as to how the operation of the center might be made self-sufficient.

One major reason for the annual deficit was that part-time employees in the food service department received benefits of full-time employees. The district and the teachers union, which also represented the cafeteria and food service workers, negotiated a settlement that maintained benefits for current employees but would not extend to future part-time employees.

The blue-ribbon panel included both local and national food service experts from private industry and the public sector. The panel's recommendations changed the operation from one of significant loss to one that, by 1990, was generating a surplus. The recommendations centered on two areas: the center facility and food service at the school level. The panel recommended that the district (a) sell unused equipment in the food service center; (b) lease to small business the excess, underused freezer capacity in the center; and (c) explore the preparation of foods for other nonprofit organizations. The board approved the implementation of these recommendations.

A fourth recommendation focused on more aggressive marketing of the food service to increase student participation in middle and secondary schools. The recommendation included offering more appealing menu items and more options. A new food service director was hired to implement the recommendations and to increase student participation. Through creative marketing techniques and a significant change in the menu offerings, the students' participation increased significantly. The director also initiated a catering service for school district functions and for a limited outside clientele. The department won the bid to provide foods for the city summer parks program and also began to service other small, private preschools as well as programs for the elderly.

The food service program quickly became a more efficient operation, and the need for annual subsidization diminished. By 1992, the department had an annual surplus in excess of $300,000. Much of the credit is due to the collaborative support of the Pittsburgh Chamber of Commerce.

Lessons Learned From Community Involvement

Through almost two decades of working with community leaders and by sharing experiences with fellow superintendents, I have learned some important lessons about community collaboration. The superintendent's role in involving community agencies in school district affairs is a crucial one. By involving the community, the superintendent

builds goodwill for the district,
uses the talent of competent people in the community to supplement that of district personnel,
provides a high-quality professional development experience for all those involved, and
produces public relations benefits by enhancing the image of the school district for those who collaborate.

For external involvement to be effective, however, it must be genuine. The school district must have a serious purpose for engaging the community, and the board of education must be willing to listen respectfully to the recommendations of study groups. If the board or the superintendent do not act on recommendations, they should make the reasons known; similarly, when the board acts on recommendations, it should keep study groups apprised of progress.

School district personnel need to be prompt and courteous when members of the private or public sector collaborate with them. Meetings must be well planned and efficiently run; busy people do not want to waste their time. The superintendent may need to maintain personal contact with individuals and study groups to demonstrate his or her concern and interest and, where necessary, to resolve problems.

Most important, superintendents and other educators who engage the public must follow through on agreements; failure to follow through in a timely manner conveys a lack of sincere interest. Last, the school district needs to join with community participants in acknowledging the successes achieved through mutual collaboration. Often, businesses or boards of education will sponsor receptions to celebrate achievements and to recognize individuals for exceptional contributions. Acknowledgement and recognition go a long way toward developing and maintaining positive working relationships.

Business and Education Collaborations
for Educational Enhancement

Exemplary collaborative relationships were forged in two school districts with their business and industrial communities. These relationships underscore the great interest and willingness of business and industry to work with schools to improve the quality of education for children and youths. Here are descriptions of the outstanding accomplishments of the Tupelo, Mississippi, school district and an effective Tech Prep Program in Palatine, Illinois.

Tupelo, Mississippi: A Culture for
Education and Economic Development

With a school district of 7,400 pupils, Tupelo, Mississippi, is located in one of the most dynamic regions of economic development in the nation (M. Walters, personal communication, March 2, 1995), situated at the southern tip of Appalachia in the Tennessee Valley Authority. Forty-two Fortune 500 companies are located in the region.

Some 40 to 50 years ago, community leaders realized that the region's economic development and quality of life required a highly effective public school system. The schools joined their human and financial resources with the business, industrial, and professional communities. A culture of support for public education has evolved that would be the envy of any school district in America. This collaboration results in the Tupelo schools receiving $750,000 of private support annually for improving educational programs for students and for professional development for teachers and administrators. The funding comes from the Hancock Learning Institute, the Association for Excellence in Education, and CREATE Foundation as well as individuals and businesses.

Hancock Learning Institute. A major source of annual revenue is the interest from a $3.5 million gift of real property to the Tupelo schools in 1991 by a local philanthropist; it is probably the single largest amount of money given to a public school district in America. The endowment generates $250,000 a year to fund the Hancock Learning Institute, a professional development facility for teachers and administrators in Tupelo.

The Association for Excellence in Education (AEE). The AEE was formed in 1983 by a group of private individuals who wanted to enhance the financial support for the Tupelo schools. It raises about $100,000 per year to support innovation in the school district. Teachers write grant applications to this organization to obtain support for original individual classroom projects.

CREATE Foundation. A community foundation, CREATE distributes the profits from the local newspaper that was bequeathed to the region; the owner of the newspaper had made a conscious effort, over the years, to educate the region on the importance of community and economic development. The annual proceeds continue to support the improvement of the quality of life in Tupelo and the surrounding area. The public schools are a major beneficiary, receiving $100,000 per year to support innovation. Corporations and individuals also donate funds for specific projects to enhance the quality of education for students.

Technology Fund

In 1995, the district began a significant fund-raising effort to provide technology for a new facility being constructed on the high school campus. A $1 million goal has been set, to be raised from the business and industrial community. The purpose is to equip the facility with the latest technology so that students will be prepared to use technology to sustain the economic development in the region.

A Culture of Support for Public Education

The partnerships in Tupelo go far beyond the provision of monies to support improvement of education for students. They embody and act on the predominant feeling in the community that a viable public education system is vital to the quality of life, the general welfare of the community, and regional economic development.

The supportive relationships between the business and industrial community and the schools in Tupelo show a mature level of collaboration that validates the contributions that each party can make to the other's well-being. Industries, for example, have brought teachers into their plants to instruct them about the principles of total quality management; they share their perspectives on a wide range of issues that may be helpful to teachers and administrators.

In Tupelo, the schools "adopt an industry," such as electronics, to help schools think through how they can improve the quality of student life and learning. This adopt-an-industry approach is in direct contrast to the "adopt-a-school" approach used in many school districts; the connection occurs to influence directly instructional improvement in the classroom. A current planning effort is exploring how the science of electronics might be incorporated into school learning. This would prepare students to learn and work in environments that will become increasingly influenced by electronics.

Industry-Education Day

For the past 18 years, the school district has conducted an industry-education day in which over 900 educators from the region meet with experts from business and industry. These meetings allow teachers to find out how they can prepare students with the knowledge and skills needed for the 21st-century workplace. The business partners help teachers make the connections between school and the workplace; an explicit goal of the program is to affect classroom instruction. For example, a current theme in the district is to work with industry to discover the kind of mathematics and science that schools should teach to meet the needs of American industry. To this end, educational professionals and business leaders will work to identify ways in which they can combine their human and financial resources to reach this goal.

School Restructuring

The Tupelo schools have been involved in a serious restructuring movement with the Center for Leadership Reform in Louisville, Kentucky.

The collaboration with business and industry is part of the reorganization of the school system so that student learning can be optimized. A major current effort is to create quality schoolwork for students to engage them fully in acquiring the knowledge and skills that will enable them to become productive members of the dynamic economic life of the region.

School site budgeting allows substantial discretion to teachers and administrators to implement innovative programs to improve the quality of education as well as new ways of measuring student achievement.

The professional development program in Tupelo goes far beyond offering training to teachers and administrators. Teachers are encouraged to visit the world of education outside Tupelo as part of their professional development. And when teachers express an interest in applying new programs to the classroom, they have financial support to assist them. The district spends more than $1,000 per year per professional to support professional development; in some years, it has reached $2,000.

Tupelo has succeeded in creating a climate of support for public education that provides an exemplary model for public and private collaboration for the common good. The entire community sees the relationship between good public education, economic development, and the quality of life. It is a model worthy of replication throughout the United States.

Palatine, Illinois: Business and the Tech Prep Program

The Northwest Suburban Career Cooperative (NWCC) in the suburbs of Chicago provides the leadership to implement tech prep career programs (P. Block, personal communication, March 2, 1995). This effective group is composed of 120 business partners, 12 large suburban high schools, and Harper Community College. In these programs, students take academic courses that meet college admission requirements; the courses are related to work-based learning and are followed by 2 years of community college work leading to an associate degree in applied science.

NWCC involves large corporations, such as Allstate Insurance, J. C. Penney, Kraft General Foods, Sears, and Xerox, as well as smaller companies. The tech prep programs include banking and insurance, drafting and computer-aided design, heating and cooling, child care, food science, and health services. The work experience for students includes summer internships. Each program was shaped by a task force of business and industry representatives, counselors, and teachers (academic and vocational) from the cooperative's member districts. The task forces identified the skills that students must acquire to function successfully in the chosen occupation. The cooperative development of curricula assures businesses that students will have the knowledge, skills, and work experience that promote effective transition and integration into the workforce.

The program has been in operation since 1990. During the early years, there was pressure to expand the program to cover as many career areas as possible. The cooperative has made a concerted effort to slow down expansion, however, and increase the quality control of existing programs. Substantial work has been done to (a) integrate classroom instruction with business experiences, (b) provide interdisciplinary curricula, and (c) strive for application of the academics in the tech prep program. The school-to-work assistance team (SWAT) represents one important measure to improve quality. The SWAT teams are composed of business people and educators, and each team works with teachers, parents, and students to prepare the high school students for career development. Each team develops its own unique way to work with its clientele to improve program quality. One school decided to create a school-within-a-school located in a precision tool company; the teachers are directly involved with the company employees in curriculum development. By the 1995-96 academic year, students will attend classes at the industrial site.

Two of the cooperative's schools developed business mentors for teachers to facilitate the development of curricula; field experiences and internships were developed to increase the program's quality for students. Because these teacher-business mentorships have been effective, they will be expanded to all schools in the NWCC.

NWCC is be commended for maintaining its current offerings, growing slowly, and focusing on quality control. This emphasis on slower growth and quality control ensures that all program components are carefully developed and that successful experiences for students, teachers, and the business community are provided.

The students' progress in the tech prep program has resulted in an important redesign effort. Most of the students still go on to postsecondary education, but the data analysis indicates three important trends: (a) Many students do not complete the program in which they started; (b) many students change direction and pursue other career choices after a year or so; and (c) most students are not satisfied with an associate degree and aspire to a baccalaureate degree.

As a result of these findings, the cooperative developed a career awareness program offered early in the high school years so that students would be more aware of career options prior to entering the tech prep programs.

The Cooperative has also changed in organizational structure. A new leadership team from the community was convened to develop a fresh school-to-work philosophy and goals. As a result, a major policy decision has been made to expand the program to provide career awareness experiences for every student in the cooperative's schools. The career development program will encompass the professions and will expand to other white- and blue-collar job opportunities.

Every student, regardless of career aspirations, will participate in job-shadowing experiences in high school and a summer internship; this will be in addition to higher-level academic courses and related technical courses in the career selected. This new program policy is anticipated to increase the quality of career decisions made by students and reduce the incidence of changes in career direction.

SUMMARY

The superintendent needs to engage the community's stakeholders to support the school district. In doing so, he or she uses the community's talent and builds constituencies to support educational programs and provide needed financial resources.

Task forces for magnet schools and for school restructuring in Pittsburgh are examples of how the community can influence education in significant ways. The magnet school task force paved the way for the district's successful desegregation plan. The restructuring task force helped to design schools for the 21st century and identified policy issues relating to the restructuring process.

Pittsburgh's Business and Finance Academy and Science and Mathematics Academy illustrate extensive community collaboration. The Business and Finance Academy was collaboratively developed with the Urban League of Pittsburgh and the banking community; it prepares students for the banking industry. The Science and Mathematics Academy exemplifies how a major national corporation can work effectively with a school district; the product was a high-quality academic program to prepare minority students for careers in math, science, and engineering.

Collaboration with the Pittsburgh Chamber of Commerce demonstrates how the business community can help to improve a district's support services—in this case, a significantly improved food service department.

Tupelo, Mississippi, provides a unique example of a community culture that views schools as part of its community development and its regional economic health. The superintendent and the business community work together to provide adequate financial support to improve the quality of schooling. The business community views effective schools as a viable economic development tool and a key to improving the quality of life for the city and the region. In turn, the schools view business as helping them offer more effective education for students. Tupelo schools adopt industries to help design more effective programming for students. A current emphasis is the use of advanced technology in the education of children. Professional development for Tupelo's teachers and administrators is heavily supported by funding from local philanthropists and the business community.

The Northwest Suburban Career Cooperative in Palatine, Illinois, demonstrates how 120 business partners, 12 school districts, and a community college collaborate in a high-quality tech prep program for the benefit of students. Quality control of the program is a hallmark of this cooperative. The integration of classroom and business experiences and a school-to-work assistance team provides career guidance for each student enrolled in the program. Currently, the cooperative is planning to offer career development programs for all students in its 12 school districts to help them make wiser career decisions.

References

Academy for Educational Development. (1985). *Teacher development in schools: A report to the Ford Foundation.* New York: Author.

Archbald, D., & Newmann, F. M. (1988). *Beyond standardized testing: Assessing authentic achievement in the secondary school.* Reston, VA: National Association of Secondary School Principals.

Atkin, J. M., & Atkin, A. (1989). *Improving science education through local alliances.* Santa Cruz, CA: Network Publication.

Bennett, C. I. (1990). *Comprehensive multicultural education: Theory and practice* (2nd ed.). Boston: Allyn & Bacon.

Bruer, J. T. (1993). *Schools for thought.* Cambridge: MIT Press.

Bryck, A. (1993). *A view from the elementary schools: The state of reform in Chicago.* Chicago: Consortium on Chicago Schools Research.

Chideya, F. (1991, December 2). The best schools in the world. *Newsweek,* pp. 50-64.

Clarkson, F., & Porteous, S. (1993). *Challenging the Christian right: The activist's handbook* (2nd ed.). Great Barrington, MA: Institute for First Amendment Studies.

202   FROM VISION TO PRACTICE

Cooley, W. W., & Bickel, W. E. (1986). *Decision-oriented educational research.* Boston: Kluwer-Nijhoff.

Edmonds, R. (1979). Effective schools for the urban poor. *Educational Leadership, 37,* 15-18.

Firestone, W. A., Rosenblum, S., & Webb, A. (1987). *Building commitment among students and teachers: An exploratory study of ten urban high schools.* Philadelphia: Research for Better Schools.

Fullan, M., & Stiegelbauer, S. (1991). *The new meaning of educational change* (2nd ed.). New York: Teachers College Press.

Gardner, H. (1983). *Frames of mind: The theory of multiple intelligences.* New York: Basic Books.

Hall, G. E., & Hord, S. M. (1987). *Change in schools: Facilitating the process.* Albany: State University of New York Press.

Hammond, P., LeMahieu, P. G., & Wallace, R. C., Jr. (1989, March). *Seeing the whole picture: The educational program audit.* Paper presented at the annual meeting of the American Educational Research Association, San Francisco, CA.

Hill, P. T., Wise, A. E., & Shapiro, L. A. (1989). *Educational progress: Cities mobilize to improve their schools.* Santa Monica, CA: RAND.

Hunter, M. (1976). *Improved instruction.* El Segundo, CA: TIP Publications.

Johnson, D. W., Johnson, R. T., & Smith, K. A. (1991). *Cooperative learning: Increasing college faculty instructional productivity.* Washington, DC: George Washington University, School of Education and Human Development.

Joyce, B., & Showers, B. (1988). *Student achievement through staff development.* London: Longman.

Kerchner, C. T., & Koppich, J. E. (1993). *A union of professionals: Labor relations and educational reform.* New York: Teachers College Press.

Lewis, A. C. (1988, September). America's ten best school programs. *Ladies Home Journal,* pp. 65-194.

Madaus, G. E. (1992). *The influence of testing on teaching math and science in grades 4-12.* Boston: Boston College, Center for the Study of Testing, Evaluation, and Educational Policy.

Nanus, B. (1992). *Visionary leadership.* San Francisco: Jossey-Bass.

Nettles, S. M., McHugh, B., & Gottfredson, G. D. (1994). *Meeting the challenges of multicultural education: The third report from the evaluation of Pittsburgh's Prospect Multicultural Education Center.* Baltimore: Johns Hopkins University, Center for Social Organization of Schools.

Newmann, F. M. (1991a). Linking restructuring to authentic student achievement. *Phi Delta Kappan, 72*(6), 458-463.

Newmann, F. M. (1991b). Promoting higher order thinking in social studies: Common indicators and diverse social studies courses. *Theory and Research in Social Education, 19*(4), 409-431.

Newmann, F. M. (1992). Classroom thoughtfulness. In F. M. Newmann (Ed.), *Student engagement and achievement in American secondary schools* (pp. 62-91). New York: Teachers College Press.

Newmann, F. M., & Wehlage, G. G. (1993). Five standards of authentic instruction. *Educational Leadership, 50*(7), 8-12.

Public Education Fund. (1993). *Imagine: The report of the PROBE Commission.* Providence, RI: Author.

Salmon-Cox, L. (1983). *The results of a survey of principals' views about PRISM.* Unpublished manuscript, University of Pittsburgh, Learning Research and Development Center.

Schorr, L. (1988). *Within our reach: Breaking the cycle of disadvantage.* New York: Anchor Press-Doubleday.

Senge, P. M. (1990). *The fifth discipline.* New York: Doubleday.

Sergiovanni, T. J. (1992). *Moral leadership: Getting to the heart of school improvement.* San Francisco: Jossey-Bass.

Simmons, W., & Resnick, L. (1993). Assessment as the catalyst of school reform. *Educational Leadership, 50*(5), 11-15.

Sizer, T. R. (1984). *Horace's compromise.* Boston: Houghton Mifflin.

Smith, W. F., & Andrews, R. L. (1989). *Instructional leadership: How principals make a difference.* Alexandria, VA: Association for Supervision and Curriculum Development.

Taylor, J. (1992, August). *Valucation: Definition, theory, and methods.* Paper presented at the Annual Convention of the Association of Black Psychologists, Denver, CO.

Twentieth Century Fund. (1992). *Report of the Twentieth Century Fund Task Force on School Governance.* New York: Author.

Wallace, R. C., Jr. (1985a). *Redirecting a school district based on the measurement of learning through examinations.* Paper presented at the annual fall conference of the Educational Testing Service, New York.

Wallace, R. C., Jr. (1985b). *The superintendent of education: Data-based educational leadership.* Pittsburgh, PA: University of Pittsburgh, Learning Research and Development Center.

Wallace, R. C., Jr. (1990). Greet the press! Candor, responsiveness pay off with reporters. *The School Administrator, 47*(7), 1-17.

204   FROM VISION TO PRACTICE

Wallace, R. C., Jr. (1993). Lessons learned from staff development in
Pittsburgh. *Journal of Staff Development, 14*(2), 4-6.

Wallace, R. C., Jr., LeMahieu, P. G., & Bickel, W. E. (1990). The Pittsburgh experience: Achieving commitment to comprehensive staff
development. In B. Joyce (Ed.), *Changing school culture through staff
development: 1990 yearbook of the Association for Supervision and
Curriculum Development* (pp. 185-202). Alexandria, VA: Association
for Supervision and Curriculum Development.

Wallace, R. C., Jr., Radvak-Shovlin, B., Piscolish, M., & LeMahieu, P. G.
(1990, April). *The instructional cabinet and shared decision making
in the Pittsburgh public schools.* Paper presented at the annual meeting
of the American Educational Research Association, Boston.

Wallace, R. C., Jr., & Reidy, E. F., Jr. (1980, June). *Respect for teachers:
The missing element in plans to improve student achievement.* Paper
presented at the Canadian Congress on Education, Montreal, Canada.

*Webster's third new international dictionary of the English language,
unabridged.* (1993). Springfield, MA: Merriam-Webster.

White, J. A., & Wehlage, G. G. (in press). Community collaboration: If it
is such a good idea, why is it so hard? *Education Evaluation and Policy
Analysis.*

Index

CORWIN
PRESS

The Corwin Press logo—a raven striding across an open book—represents the happy union of courage and learning. We are a professional-level publisher of books and journals for K-12 educators, and we are committed to creating and providing resources that embody these qualities. Corwin's motto is "Success for All Learners."